How to take great photographs with your iPhone

Tips to make you a better photographer.

purposes only and is universal as so.

Table of Contents

Why Read This Book?

If you are new to photography, or you have been at it for years, taking photos with an iPhone or iPad is different from with an SLR or with a point and shoot camera.

Many of the tips throughout this book are covering photography that is the same for any way you take pictures. There are many tips also that are things you need to do on your iPhone or other phone camera to get the best possible shots from a phone camera.

These tips will also work with an android phone or android tablet. The differences are not going to affect you getting great photos with android device. Most of the apps I use are available for Android as well.

The main reason you should learn to take the best photos you can with your iPhone is that you will have it with you all the time. Having a camera with you when the right time arises will make you more likely to get many shots you would have missed.

In this book, I am going to go over.

- What settings to use on your phone
- What apps to use to get the best results
- What mistakes to avoid
- General photography tips and phone camera tips
- Composition
- Street photography
- Shooting landscapes
- Shooting Portraits
- Shooting Nature shots
- Techniques for different types of shots
- Specialty types of shots
- Attachments that you can use to help improve your shots
- How to best edit your photos
- Some inspiring photos taken with iPhone

When you finish this book, you will have the knowledge and the tips to take great shots with your iPhone. People will look at them and say WOW.

I have been taking photos with passion since the late 1980s. I have over 300,000 digital pictures stored now that I have taken since that time. I also have many thousands of film pictures.

I have done several weddings and taken several photography courses over the years. I have also read thousands of books and articles on photography, and how to make your photos the best.

Experience is the main thing that will make you a better photographer. To get the right experience, you need to know the things to practice getting beyond the level you want to be.

Learning to be a great photographer is within the reach of anyone who wants to do it.

The market for small cameras and even DSLRs is decreasing because phone cameras have gotten so good. They are to the point where they are good enough to take great shots of most of what people love to take pictures of.

If you think, you have gotten good information out of the book, I would be grateful if you went to the Amazon site and leave a review.

I have a couple of other photography books; I think you may enjoy.

Digital landscape photography projects to make you a better photographer.

 Portrait photography tips to make you a better photographer.

Camera Settings

As with all photography, light is critical to taking great photos. Everyone has taken shots that are so dark you have a hard time seeing what you are taking a shot of. With all photography, light is critical to taking great photos.

On the newer iPhones, Apple has done something to make taking shots in low light much easier. We will talk about that later in the book. It is extremely exciting.

We will talk about how you can use some simple settings on your phone. They will work when you are taking the shots, and your pictures will be better.

The quickest and easiest setting you can change is setting the exposure.

Open the camera app and tap the screen to bring up the focus point. From there, touch the little sun symbol. Move your finger toward the top of the phone to make it brighter, and down toward the bottom to make it darker.

This is important unless you already have great light for the shot. Having perfect light for the shot will mean that you are shooting with the sun at your back or from the side and back.

This is another quick and easy setting you can do before you shoot. Hold your finger on the spot until the camera locks the exposure and focuses on that spot.

This will lock in the exposure and the focus on a particular spot in the photo where the subject is. This is especially useful in portraits. You want to have the best lighting and perfect focus on the subjects face and eyes.

Do not forget to check and set the shooting mode on your camera before you take the shot. You do not want to have it on square if you are taking a shot for a wide computer screen.

You also should use the panorama mode if you want to capture an area that is wider than what fits on the screen.

Do not forget about the other phone camera settings. There is an HDR setting that will help make many of your photos better just by using it.

Take one each way or even a couple, you can delete it if you do not like it. You will never be able to take it again the same.

When you use the HDR setting on the camera, it is important to hold it very still. The camera will take 3 shots. 1 shot at the metered exposure, 1 shot with higher exposure and 1 shot with lower exposure.

Then the camera combines all 3 into one photo that will most of the time make it better than a single shot. Because it is taking three shots, it takes three times longer, so you need to hold it still for the whole time.

This is not really a camera setting; it is more about camera holding. How you hold your phone, and how steady you are when you hit the shutter button will have a big effect on how good your pictures are.

Try to hold the camera as steady as you can when you are about to take the shot. The lower the light levels, the more movement will affect your shots. Try to steady the phone on or against something. If you do not have a tripod, there are still many things you can do.

You can support your hands-on something like a fence, railing, a tree branch, etc. You can even lean against a tree or a wall. Anything you can do to steady the shot will get you better pictures.

One thing I do often is set the phones on something, set it up for the shot, and take the shot with my Bluetooth shutter button. It is a great investment in getting you better shots.

Another method that helps is to use image stabilization that is part of some phone camera apps. Apps like Camera +, one of the apps I use quite a bit.

Here are a few more tips that you can do with your iPhone that you may not have known.

• You can open your camera from the lock screen by sweeping up from the bottom of the screen. Great if you need to take a shot quick.
• Hold down the volume button or hold your finger on the shutter button when in the camera mode and it will go into burst mode for as long as you hold it down.
• The slow motions option is kind of cool as well. If you use this, the camera shoots at 120 frames/sec. When you play it back it plays at 30

frames/sec, so it looks like it is moving at 1/4 speed. You can also change where the slow motions effect happens by moving the black bars at the bottom of the screen in the edit mode.

- Another cool tip is to turn the phone upside down, with the lens at the bottom; you will get a slightly different angle and you can create some cool shots.

Camera apps

The first app I want to tell you about is not technically a camera app. It is one of the best most useful apps I have found to use with your camera phone. The app is <u>called Office Lens.</u> What is so great about this app is that it senses what you are taking a picture of, be it a business card, a document, a picture, etc.

The reasons I am including this app are. You can save anything paper very easily that you want to save. If you use it with Evernote, there is no limit to the things you can save. Save for further use, or to remember.

I use it when I am shopping, and I see something I want to remember. I even use it to take pictures of things on my computer screen to save for later. It is so versatile and so useful.

Here is a small example of how good it works. This is the front and back side of a gospel tract that I had sitting on the desk. The program automatically cropped it and took a good enough picture of it that made the small print easily readable. This card is business card size and the print on the back is small, yet readable.

You can do this with just about anything, and it is a great time saver. There are many other scanner apps that you can use. This one is free and works well.

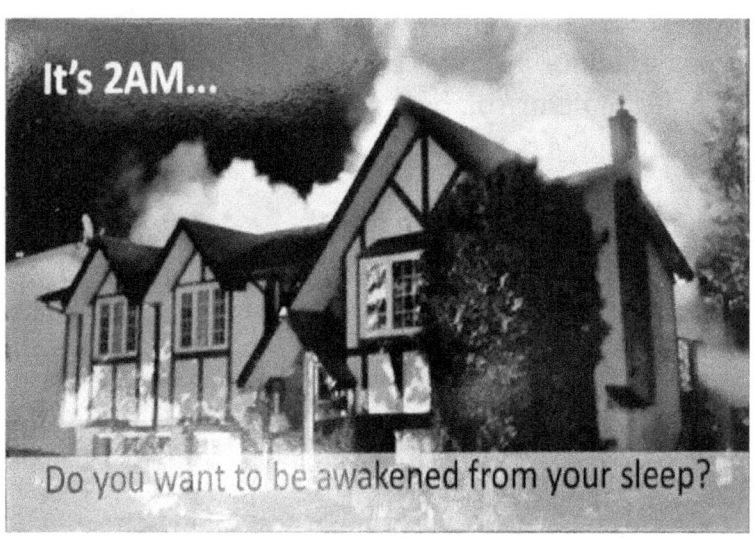

It's 2AM...

Do you want to be awakened from your sleep?

The next app and the one that you will use most of the time for taking your photos, it is the camera app that comes with your iPhone. This is the easiest and fastest camera access you have. You can access it from swiping up from the bottom of the screen, even if your phone is not unlocked. You can get to it quick.

To make it the easiest to use, I recommend keeping it set to photo instead of square and have the HDR on. This is where you will use it most. If you have more time to set up the shot, then there are other apps that will give you better results.

The first three parts of the app are for video. The other three are for photos. Use the photo mode for most shots. If you are shooting only for Instagram and you want to get a quick shot and get it on Instagram right away, use the square mode. The square mode does cut the pixels, so if you do not want to use it just for Instagram, shoot in photo mode and crop if you want to put it on Instagram.

The panorama mode works great if you want to shoot wide. You can also use the panorama mode to shoot up and down and cover more area. The panorama mode works well on the older iPhones. It has been improved so it works fantastic on the newer phones.

Go through all the features of the app and learn to use them. Learn what you can do with the app to get the most out of it.

Another fun app that will give you some great shots is an app called Photosynth. This app is no longer available. It was made by Microsoft research lab. I cannot find another app that is anywhere near as good as this one. I left it on here hoping it will come back. The app is made for taking 3d shots where you walk all around an object to get a full 360-degree photo. You can use this app to get some cool 360-degree photos, but they are not practical for most things. The panorama shots you can make with this program are very usable though.

 I like to use it for making big cool panorama shots. Take several shots of the area you want, go up and down and fill in the whole area. When you finish, you get a cool panorama.

This is a shot of the lake at the cabin that I made with Photosynth and cropped off all the excess. The shot covers about 60 feet across with lots of resolution to make some cool shots.

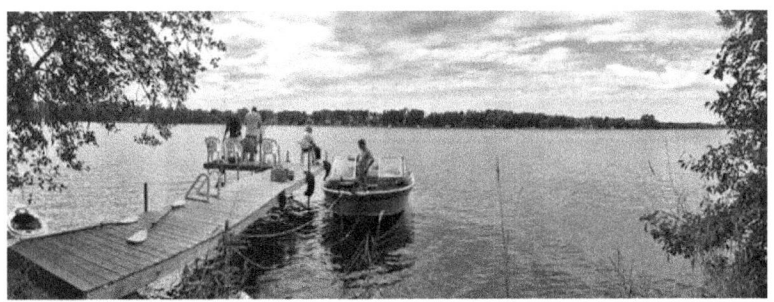

Goggle photo is a great app, especially if you take lots of pictures. One of the problems with taking a lot of pictures on your phone is you run out of storage space on the phone. Google photos will automatically upload the pictures to their storage servers for you.

There are two options for resolution. The lower resolution is free for unlimited. The higher resolution does have a charge. I even uploaded all my pictures that I have saved on my devices at home, to their servers. I have over 300,000 shots quickly available anytime, and anywhere.

Google photo also has some way to sort the shots by what it sees in the photos. It is not perfect, but it works very well. I can search for lakes, for example, and it will pull up thousands of pictures of lakes I have taken, in just a few seconds.

This is an app everyone needs to have.

Camera + is the photo app that I use a lot of the time, if I have time to set up the shot, otherwise like I said, I use the Apple camera app. The camera + is an app that you take the picture with the app, and then you can do all the editing to make it the best possible shot, within the app as well.

You do not have to edit it right away, which is nice; you can do it when you get time to do it. The app keeps the shots inside the app until you edit them and save them to your camera roll, or somewhere else.

This app is excellent if you are accustomed to taking your photos with an SLR, or a point and shoot. It is also a great app to learn from if you want to learn to use an SLR. The app shows you the aperture and shutter speed and lets you adjust it. It also lets you touch the screen and lock the focus and exposure where you want it.

It has a grid on the screen to allow you to set up your composition like you want, and has a leveling line, so you can get the horizon straight with no trouble.

You can set it for shutter priority or full manual as well. It also has a macro setting, and image stabilization, a timer, and burst mode. The macro setting is good for getting in close. Even closer than you can get with the Apple camera app.

After you take the shots, you tap on the flower looking symbol in the lower left corner. When you do this, you tap on the shot you want to fix, and it opens the editing part of the app, where you have literally hundreds of options to make the shots look better.

The app comes in a free version which is particularly good, but the pro version is well worth the small charge. In the pro version, you have access to a section that is called the lab. In the free version you can use many of the editing tools with the normal settings. In the lab section, you can adjust the settings to what you feel is a good setting.

One other thing I feel is important about this app that some of the others cannot do is edit without a phone internet connection. When I am at the cabin and taking shots, I can edit them on the phone. I do not get service all the places at the cabin. Some of the other apps I have used have to have a connection to cell towers or wi-fi to be able to edit the shots, because they are online apps.

Here is a link to their iTunes app

This link if for the legacy version. There is a newer app, Camera+2 that is much more in-depth, but the legacy version is still quite good.

Here is a quick example of what one little tap can do to make your shots look so much better. The first shot is from the iPhone camera app; the second shot is with the Camera+ with a slight tweak of the clarify adjustment.

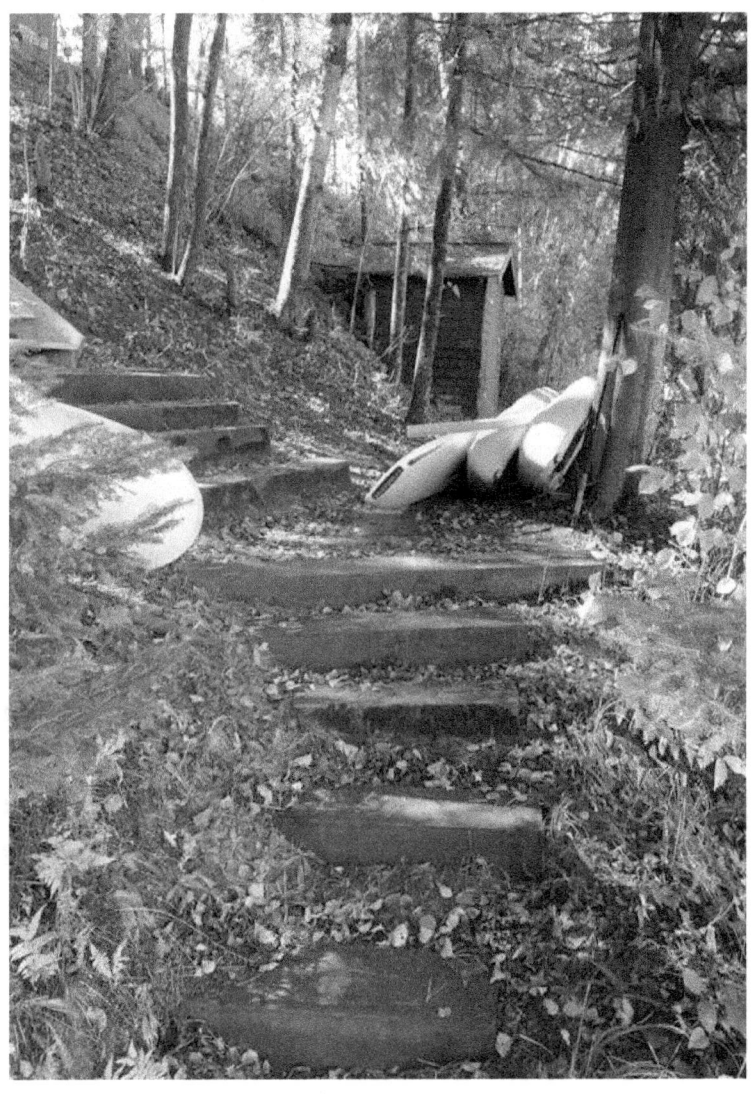

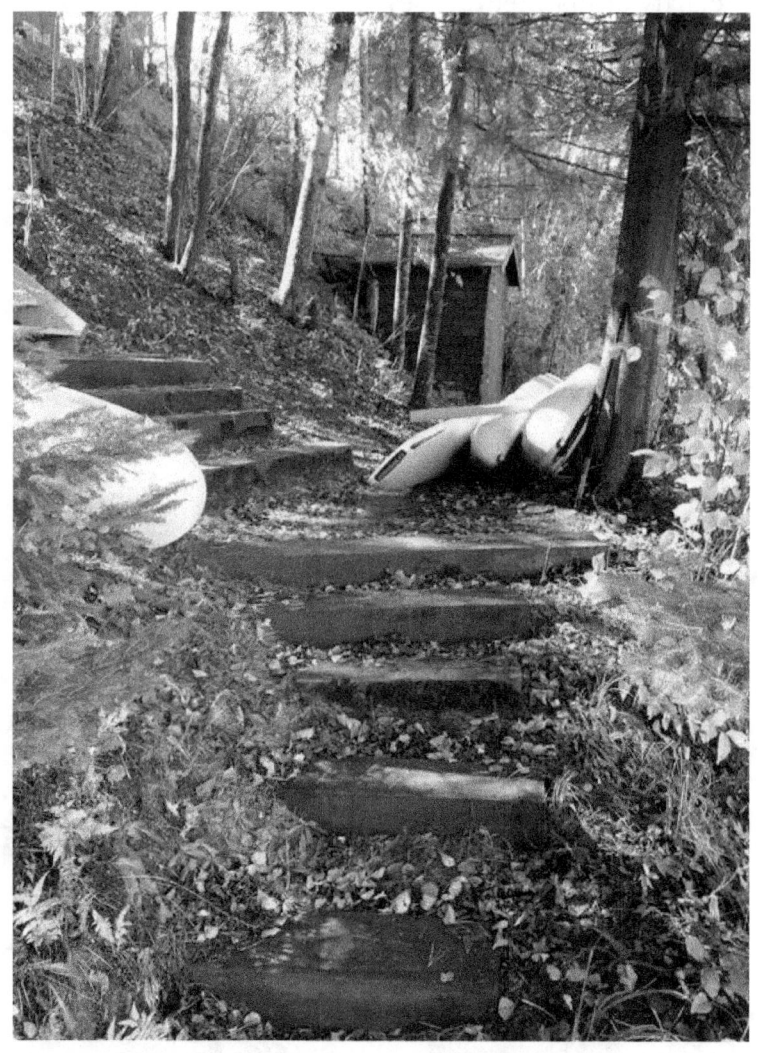

There is not a big difference, but the extra crispness and colors make the photo pop.

Another app that is a good camera app. Be funky

I have used this app many times. The app works well and has many great features as part of it. You can edit in the app after you take the shot. It has a quick easy editor that you can make nice photos with a couple clicks. To get a nice quick edit, open the app, click on photo editor. Select the photo and click on the edits in the lower section and click on beautify. It will instantly make your shop better.

This app has several other things you can do. It makes quite good collages as well. The editing parts are not as good as Camera +, but the beautify setting makes most shot look good.

The app is free and is an alternative to the iPhone app; it is well worth using and getting. Just go to the app store and type in be funky.

There are many more camera apps you can get. If you have an iPhone 10 or newer, the Apple app is great for most anything you want to do. If you like making art like photos, there are great apps for that.

Black and White apps

Some of the best black and white conversions are available on apps on your phone. If you want to learn to see the best looks, convert to black and white with phone apps. I have 3 favorite apps I use.

One of my favorites is Enlight for converting. This app changed to photo fox and now it is photo leap. It is a great app, but the price keeps going up. You can get a free trial on it to see if you like it. My favorite for shooting black and white with your phone is an app called Dramatic black and white. Dramatic costs $4.99, well worth it. You can make the same shots with the apps, but it takes work in a photo editor.

Here is a shot I took at the cabin using the Dramatic app. I think it can take a nothing boring picture and subject and makes it an interesting shot. Just because of the tones and the big contrast.

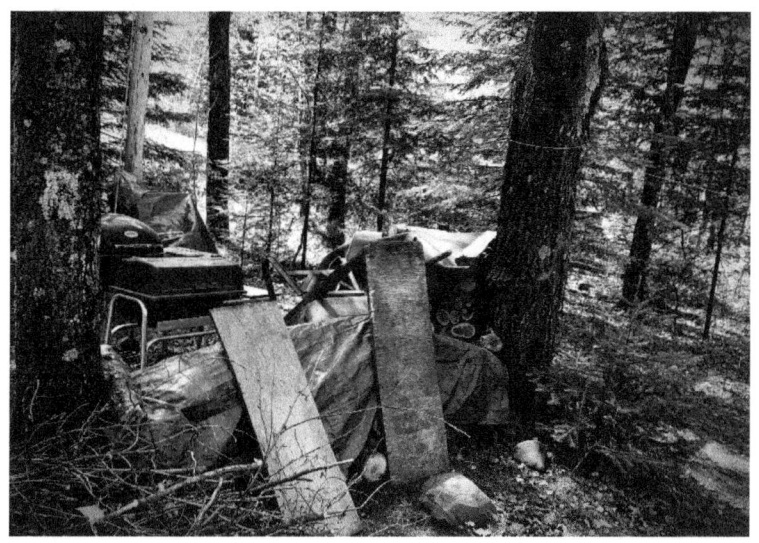

Argentum camera is another black and white app that is useful. This one is free. It does a good job with black and white shots. The best thing about this app is that it lets you see the scene and compose it without the color distracting from what you see. It has the fewest features, but it does work well. They have filters you can buy but you get one free and it works well.

These are the 2 best apps I have found for taking shots in black and white.

The best apps for converting color shots to black and white.

Argentum, the app I mentioned above that lets you take shots seeing them in black and white. This can be an advantage because you can see the contrast and you can see the light and shadows better than in color.

Dramatic black and white. This is the other app I would recommend. One of the big differences between the apps is dramatic black and white uses your camera app on your phone. It is a cool option with the iPhone 7 plus and newer, you can use all the cool camera features of the iPhone 7 plus and newer. If I had to have only one, this would be the one.

Mistakes to Avoid.

● **Not having a focal point.** Not having a subject that the viewer can easily see is why you took the shot. This is one of the biggest problems that people have with snapshots and travel shots. Here is an example of not having a subject or main focal point. Even though this is a beautiful spot, what is the subject?

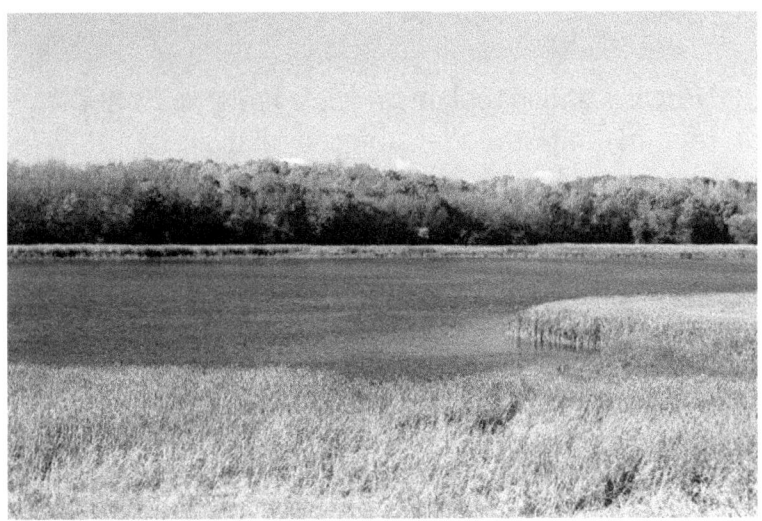

Is it the fall colors, or the lake, or the cattails? It is not clear. Sometimes shots like this are ok, but you want to have a clear subject to have a great shot.

● **Having the subject out of focus**. If you take the shot quick and are not paying attention to where the camera is focusing, you can ruin the shot by having some other part of the shot in focus instead of the subject. The camera normally does a good job, but to be safe, use the focus lock to make sure.

Here is a shot I took of an icicle hanging from the roof, making sure the subject is sharp. The background being out of focus is good. The icicle almost looks like its aluminum because of the lighting.

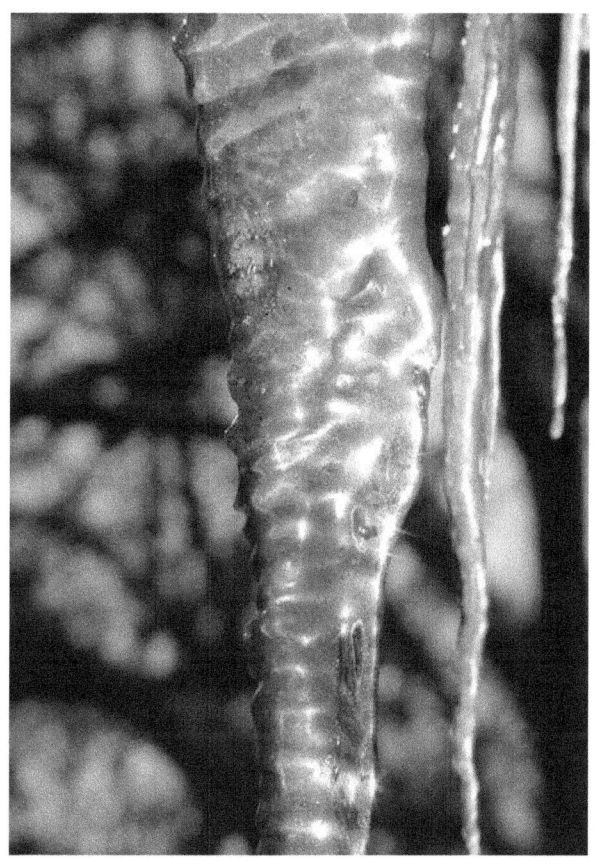

● **Over or underexposure.** I see a lot of photos that people take and the subject is not exposed correctly, generally to dark. One of the biggest mistakes people make is having bright sky for the background. The subject is dark. This is especially bad with shots of people.

Here is a shot of my wife with her catch, when I looked to take the shot facing the lake, she was way too dark; we turned around with the shoreline as the background. This was a quick shot just to get the fish, not the best, but I wanted to get the fish in the water.

Make sure you look at the lighting on the subject. Looking the other direction, she would have been too dark to see the fish or her.

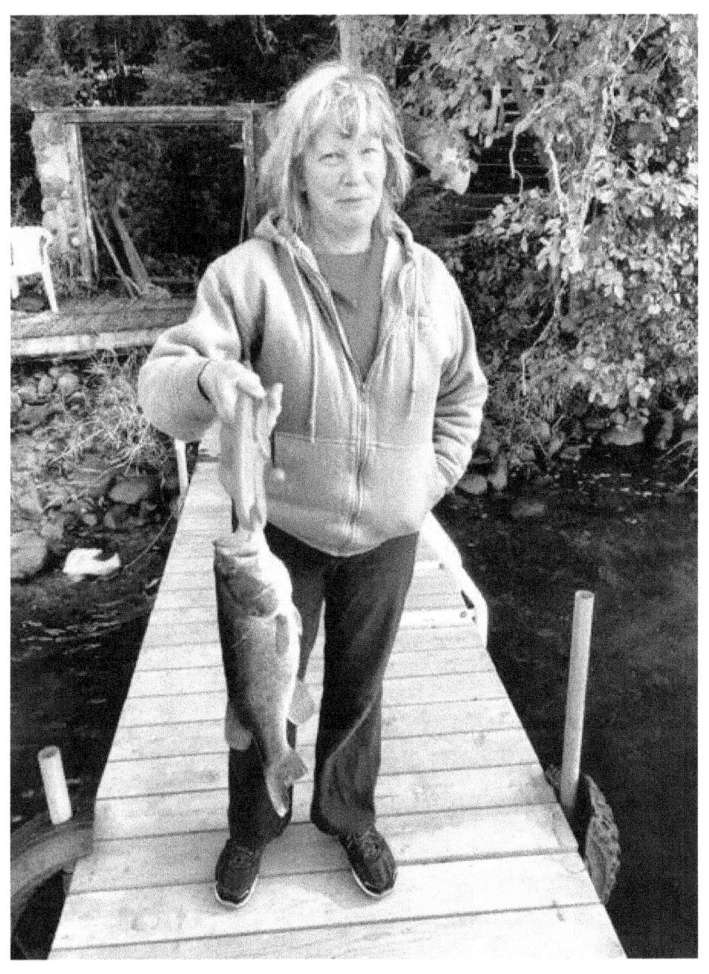

● **Blurry shots**, because of camera shake or pushing the shutter release too hard. Getting blurry shots is something that is quite easy to do, especially when taking photos in low light. You can use a tripod or some other way to steady the shot to keep it sharper. Another thing I like to use is the **Bluetooth remote** I talk about later in the book. Also use one of the apps that have image stabilization. Another option is to get the camera to use a faster shutter speed. One of the cool new features on the iPhone is being able to use the flashlight mode in camera+, to light up the subject in low light, without using the flash. On the newer iPhones, the 11 and newer, there is a fantastic low light option on this phone. I talked about it earlier in the book. Use it when shooting where there is not great light. It is better than flash because it is even lighting.

Here are two shots I took in the living room, just to show you the difference. The first one is with just the camera and aquarium lighting. The second is in flashlight mode. Not bad.

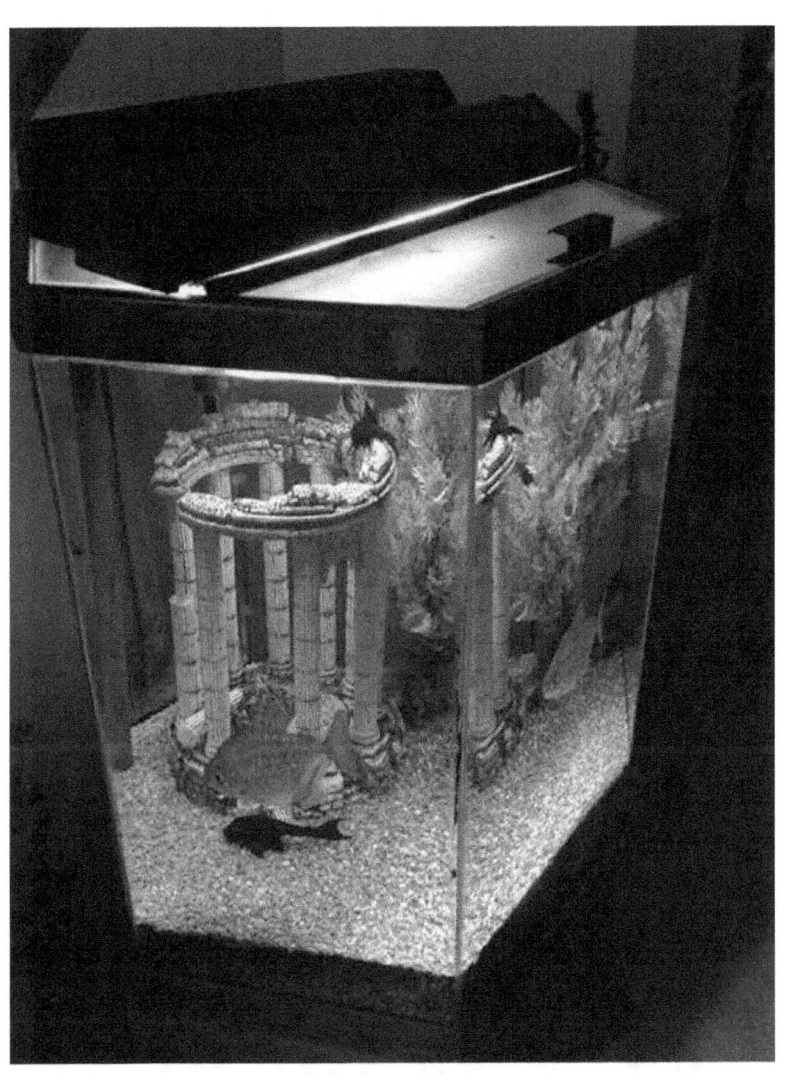

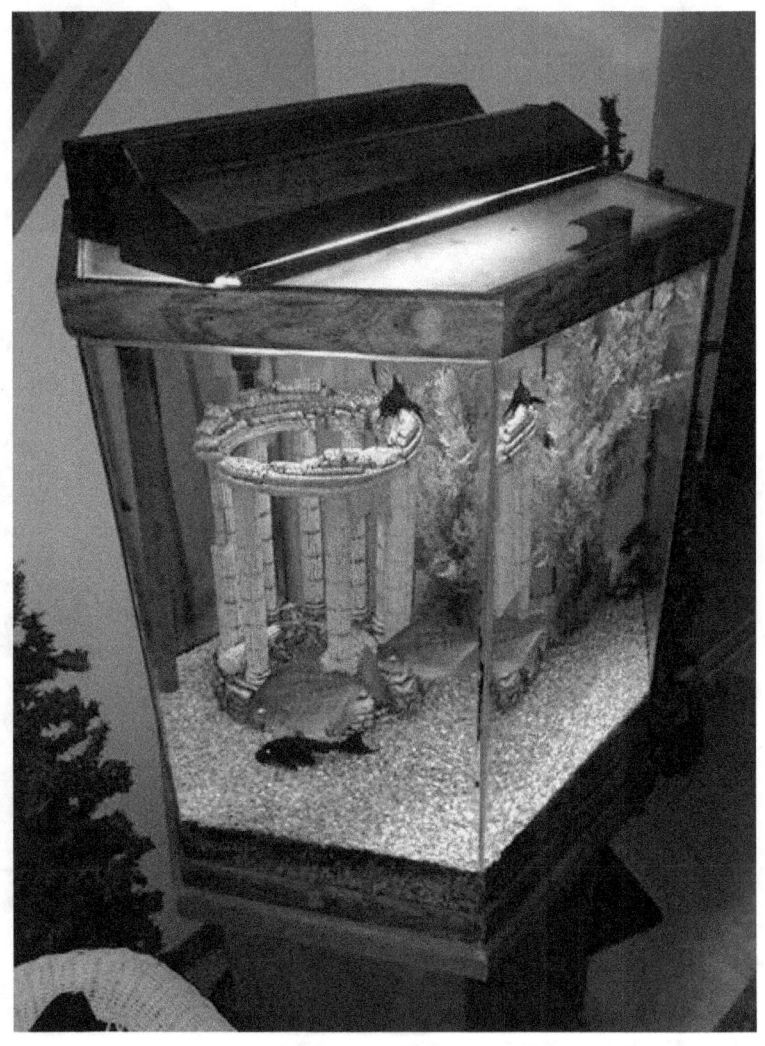

It is easy to see the difference it makes. The shot is clearer, and the lighting is better, and it brightens up the wall and surrounding area. And because it is a constant light, there are no blown out areas, or reflections on the glass.

● **Bad composition of the shot.** Having the subject dead center of the shot is a common thing for people who take snapshots to do. Generally, it is not the best way to compose the shot. Use the rule of thirds in many of your shots. At least do not overlook it.

● **Lots of clutter in the background.** Try to keep the shot as clean and simple as you can. Do not have any distracting things in the shot. Change the angle or level or something so you get a cleaner looking shot. Or get close. In the shot below, I got in close, and moved around so the shot of the apple blossoms was against the blue sky for better contrast and no distractions in the shot.

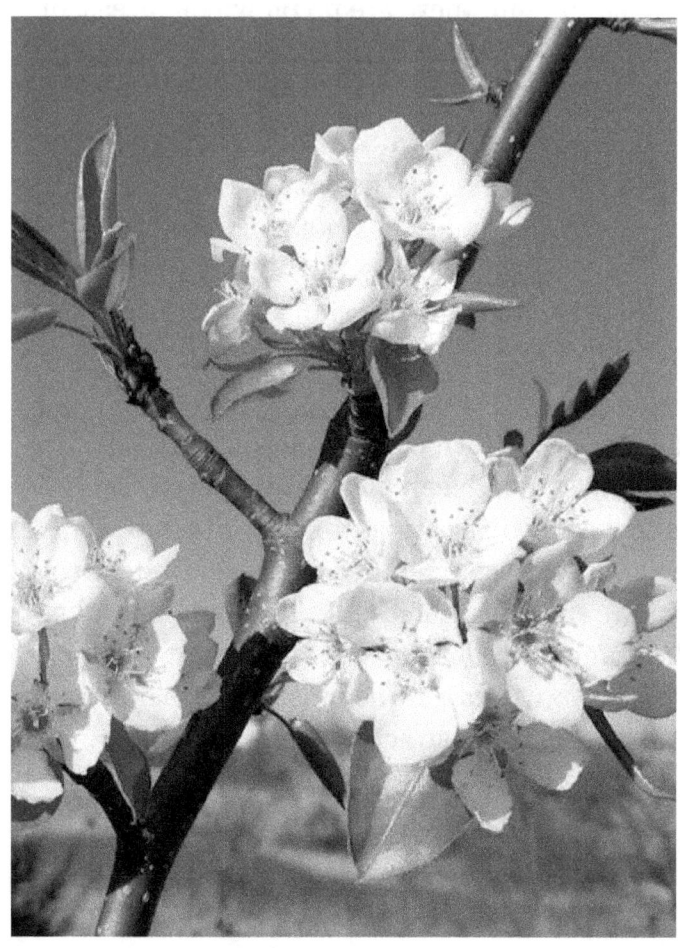

● **Do not use digital zoom.** If you do use it, just know that you are going to degrade the picture. If possible, zoom with your feet. Get closer to the subject if you can. This is mostly the best choice. The digital zoom on the iPhone 11 is extremely good, even at 5x zoom. I would not use it for a shot you want to print, but if it is for the internet it will be fine using the digital zoom.

● **Do not over edit the shot.** HDR can look cool and can make your shots better, within reason. Be careful when you edit, do not overdo it. It makes the shot look fake and bad.

General Tips

If you need to access your phone quick before you miss a great shot, you can get to it best by just hitting the home button and swiping up from the bottom. You do not even have to unlock your phone to be able to grab a quick picture.

Make sure you turn on the grid. One of the best ways to use the rule of thirds and to keep the horizon strait is to use the grid and keep everything lined up. To turn on the grid, go to your settings, go down to photos and camera, and then go down to grid and turn it on. It will help you get better shots, no matter how long you have been taking photos. It gives you a grid to line up the subject with.

Using the grid also gives you the intersections to use the rule of thirds. This is a long-time photography rule that will make your photos more enjoyable most of the time. Put the subject of your photo on one of the four crossing points of the lines.

If you are shooting a moving subject or there is movement in the scene, use the burst mode on the phone. Go into phone setting and set to use volume up as burst mode. It is fast. Hold your finger on the button to take the pictures and let it take 3 or 4 shots or more.

Use the volume button to take the shot. You can sometimes take the shot easier with either of the volume buttons than hitting the shutter button on the screen. You can also do burst mode with the volume buttons. Either of the volume buttons will do the same thing.

If you are using headphones that have a volume up and down on the cord, you can also take pictures with the volume controls on the cord. This is a great way to avoid camera movement when shooting. A Bluetooth remote is also extremely useful. We will get into that later in the book.

Try to avoid using the digital zoom. Most camera apps have it, and it is something you will need to use sometimes. Using it degrades your photos so do not use if you do not have to. If you need to get closer to the subject and if it is at all possible, get closer by moving closer to the subject, your photos will be much better. I know I mentioned this before, but it is important. Like I said before, the digital zoom on the newer phones is much better than it was before.

The other option that is better than the zoom is to take the shot at the normal lens, then crop it later to get the shot you want. This will give you the full shot to work with and you will keep more pixels in the photo than using the digital zoom.

When shooting in low light conditions, try to use natural light as much as you can. Leave the flash off most of the time.

One thing you may have not known, the iPhone saves your deleted photos for 30 days after deleting them. Go to your photo viewing app. Tap on the album symbol at the bottom of the screen, select recently deleted to see your deleted photos.

You can recover a shot you deleted accidentally, but you will also be able to see photos that you may have wanted to never be seen, make sure you delete them for good.

You can also hide photos that you may not want others to see. Select the photo and tap on the share icon. When the screen pops up, select the hide option in the lower part.

You can also do some limited editing from the photo app directly. Select the photo and select edit from the top of the photo. You can do some limited editing from here. The editing you can do has also gotten better on the newer phones. You can do quite a bit of editing to get your shots looking better.

Composition Tips

Composition on your phone camera will be the same as with any other camera. The same tips will be the same, except if you are taking shots for Instagram, Instagram shots are different because the photos that Instagram shows are square.

You can put shots on Instagram that are not square, and it will make them square to fit. One thing cool about the iPhone is that it has a square mode so you can take your shots specifically for Instagram and they will look great when you put them up, and nothing will be cut off.

One of the downsides of shooting using the square mode is that you get fewer pixels in your shot. Another option is to shoot in landscape mode and crop the shot after.

Some tips to get great square photos.

Put your subject in the center of the shot. I know this is not normal for good composition, but square changes that. If the subject is small, it is still a good idea to use the rule of thirds and do not put the subject in the center.

One other thing that works well in square photos is to look at the squares of the grid for using the rule of thirds. Pick one of the 9 squares and put the subject in that square. Generally, avoid using the center square, unless you have a strong subject that can take advantage of the center square.

If you have a shot that will look great with empty space, set it up with the grid using the rule of thirds and place the subject into one of the squares.

Fill as much of the frame as you can with the subject.

Another technique that works well with square shots is diagonals. If you have multiple subjects, put them diagonally across the picture for a more pleasant look.

Using leading lines also is amazingly effective in square shots. In normal photos leading lines leading from the lower left to upper right tend to work best. In square shots you may not be able to get the lines leading from the best direction but use them if they are effective for your shot.

Sometimes try things that break all the composition rules you can get some great and interesting shots doing everything wrong.

One of the most important tips to remember in composition is that your photograph has a main subject, or a main focal point. It is important that the viewer's eyes are drawn to the main focal point or subject of the shot.

When someone who does not know anything about the photo looks at it, you want them to know what the main subject is and why you took the shot. What were you trying to portray?

Shooting from a low angle can also add a different perspective to the shot and give the same old shots, a whole different and interesting look.

Include depth in your shots to make them better. Shooting flat subjects is not a bad thing but having depth in your shots makes them more interesting most of the time.

Keep your shots simple. Do not have anything in the shot that does not add to the photo. This is one of the most important parts of composition.

You do not want objects to distract from the subject of your photo.

Change your location and change your angle to get the best shot. There are, especially in landscape shots places that are truly spectacular, but it is hard to capture in a photo.

The key to making the photo look spectacular as well is to get the right angle and have the proper surrounding objects to make it breathtaking. Here is a shot that I took of my wife fishing. I moved around until I found the best angle and height to get the best shot.

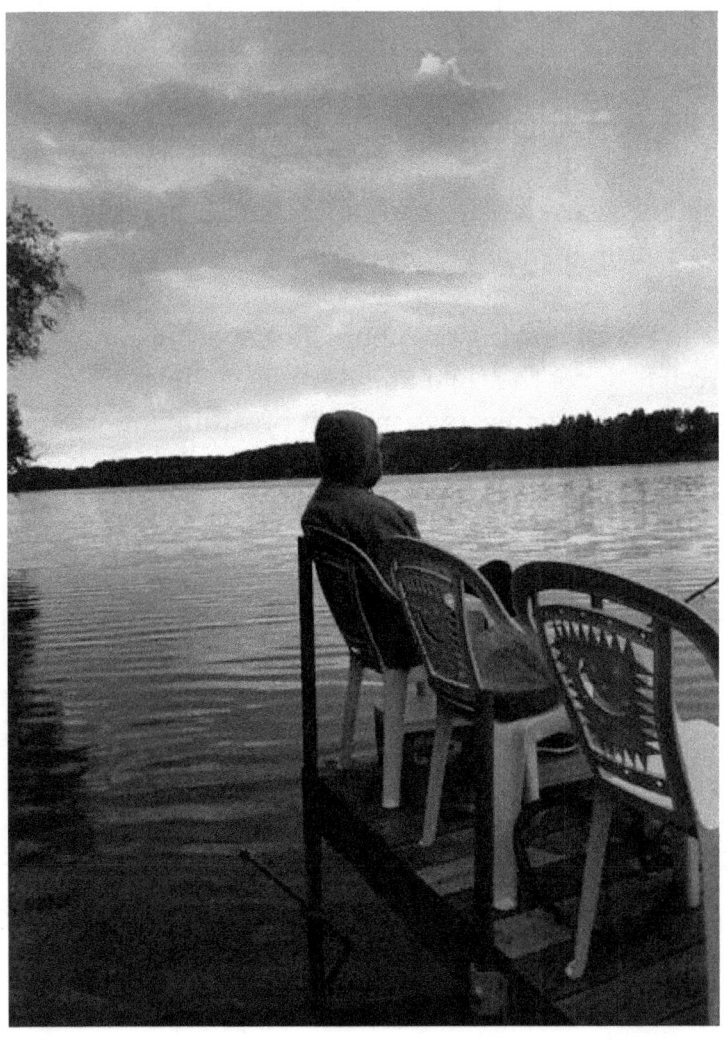

I broke the rule of thirds with this shot because I wanted to get the end of the tree branches in the shot for a little extra.

Add Depth to the shot

This is a great way to make your shots look better. If you can create a sense of depth, the photo will look more real and 3 dimensional. A flat looking shot will look lifeless and boring. The shot above also shows depth with the chairs, the trees, and the dock.

Little changes can make a big difference. All you need to do many times is to change the viewpoint of the shot or include an element in the foreground to add depth.

Here are some great techniques to add depth to your shots.

• **Use leading lines**. If you use leading lines, it will show depth because the leading lines are pulling you into the shot. The leading lines need to go from the bottom of the shots edge and converge into the distance.

Here the dock leads your eyes right to the sunset. You have no choice but to look right where I want you to look.

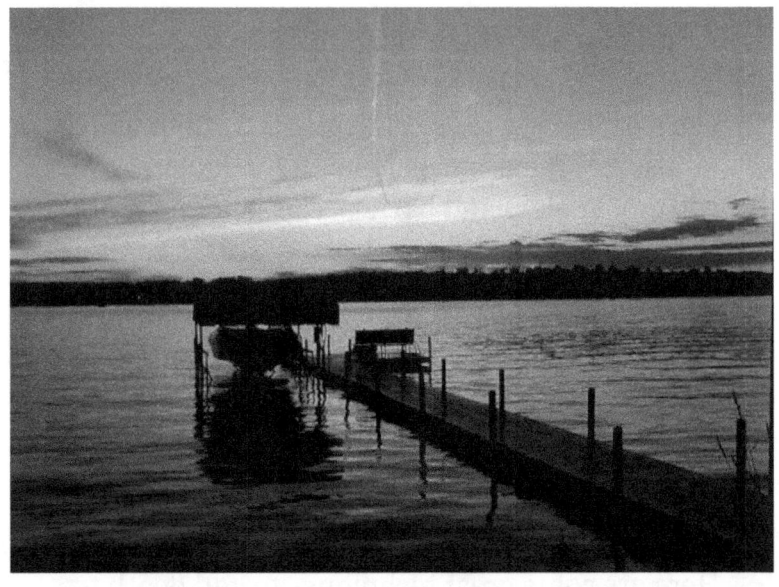

The second technique to add depth is to show something interesting in the foreground of the shot.

Here is a shot I took at Split Rock Lighthouse. The rock in the foreground is not much of a rock. But it does add depth to the shot. You can see that the rock is much closer than the lighthouse.

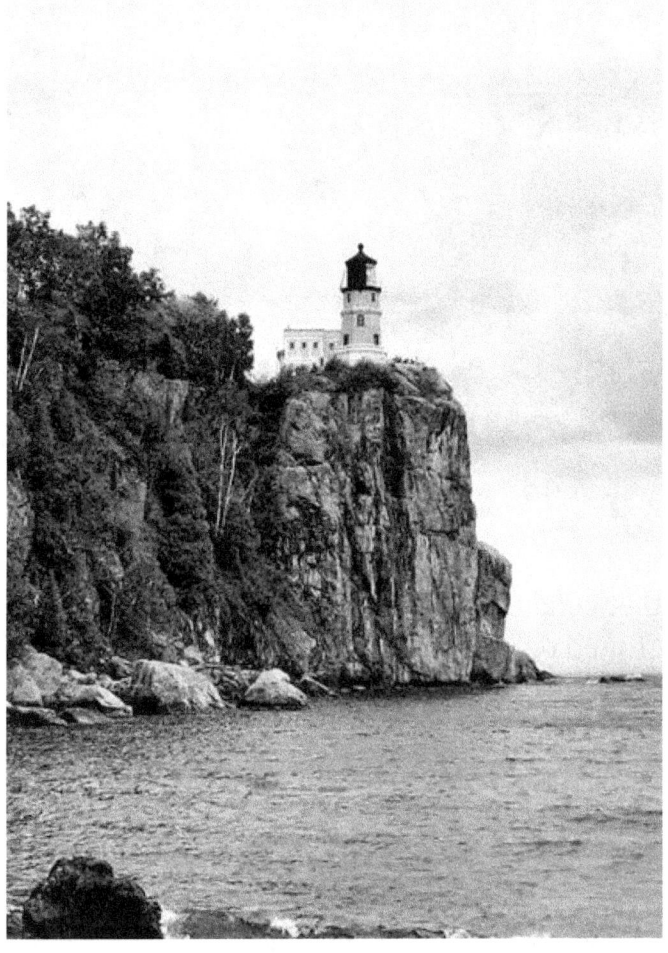

Third technique to add depth is to shoot from a low angle. This adds depth because of a foreground interest as well as creating a more exaggerated perspective.

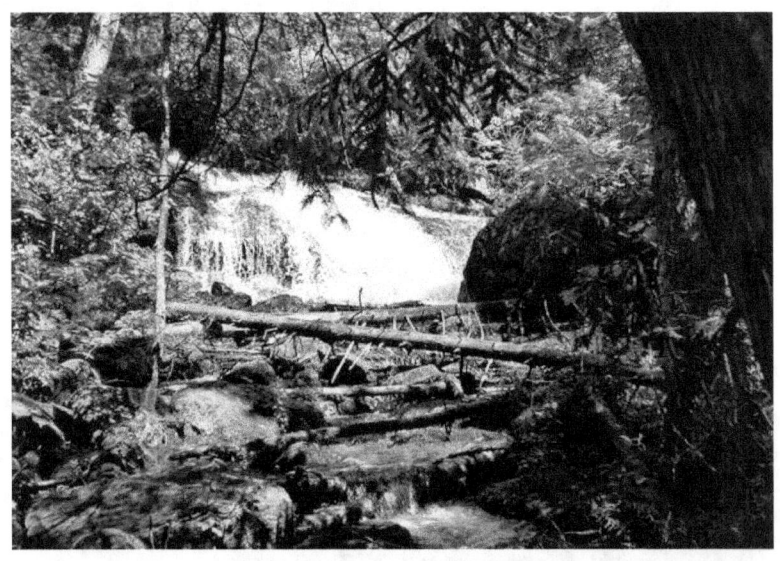

Another good technique is to frame the object with foreground objects. It does not have to be at the bottom edge of the shot, just frame the subject.

This next shot uses all the techniques in one shot. Leading lines, foreground objects, low angle and the shot is framed by the woods and rocks. It is also one of my favorite places to take photos. This is the Kettle River in Banning State Park.

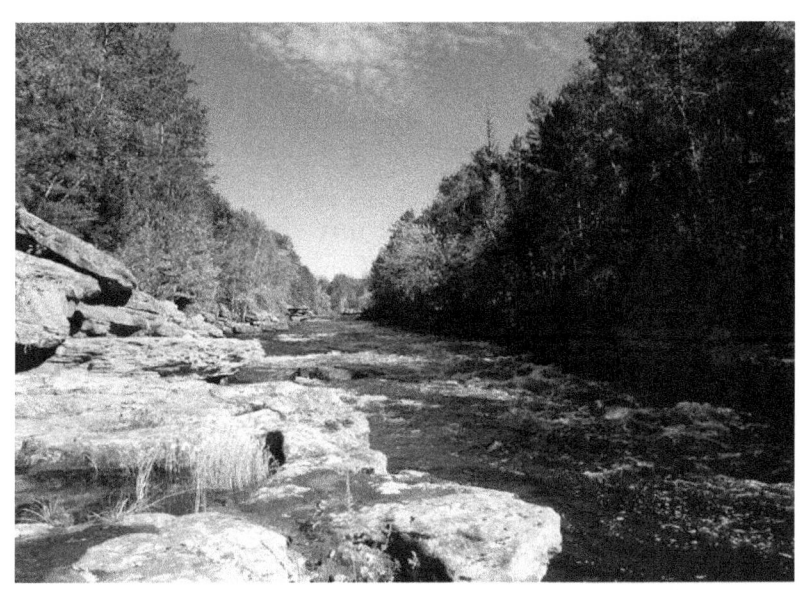

Street Photography

Street photography does not mean that you are on the street in a big city. It can be that, but street photography as I see it is anywhere you are taking shots that is outdoors, but you are not taking landscape or nature shots. That would be buildings, interesting structures, people doing things that are interesting in public, etc.

Cool building or parts of buildings that look cool are some of my favorites. I love to photograph cool looking churches and barns. Wooden barns are very cool and will most likely be extinct in the next 50 years or so. Many of the ones left are falling, and most barns now are made of metal.

Here is one of my favorite barns that I have taken pictures of. This barn is in Giese MN.

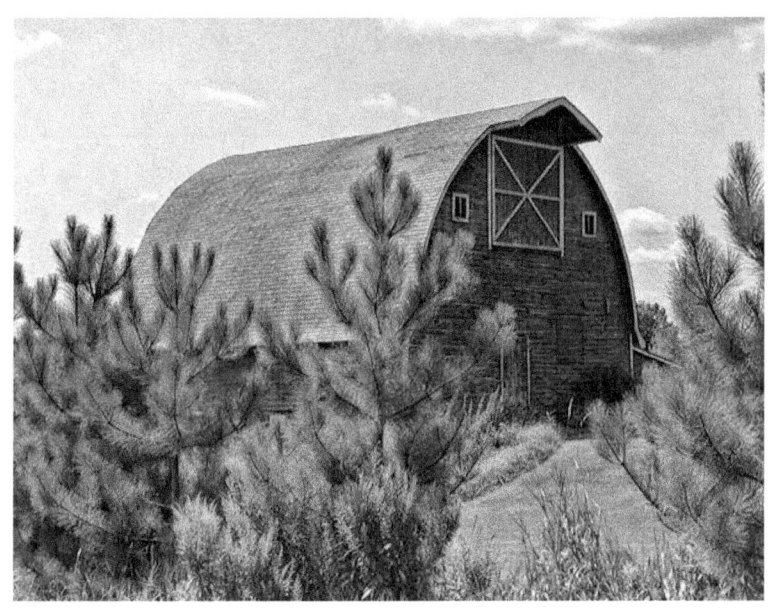

Here is another of my favorites that is off Hwy 8
near Center City MN.

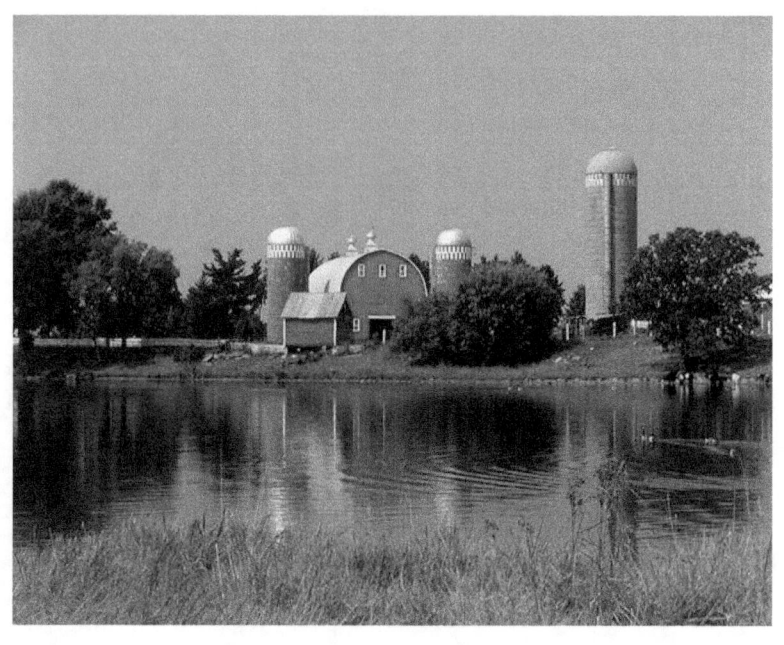

Here is just an example of a cool church shot I took.

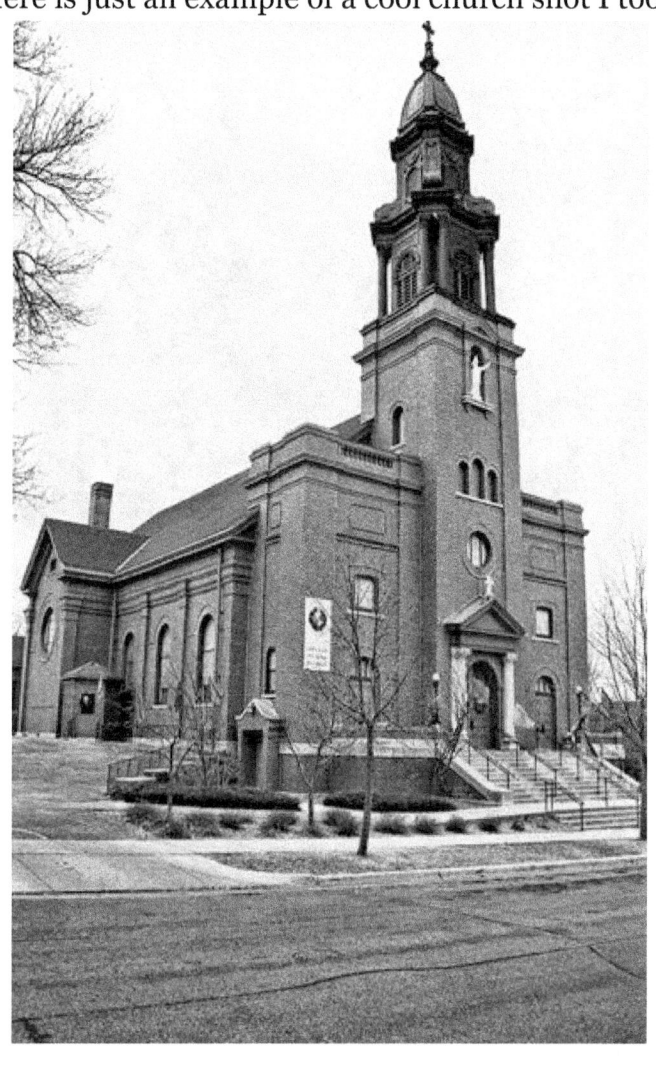

Here is a shot of the old Ramsey town hall in Ramsey MN.

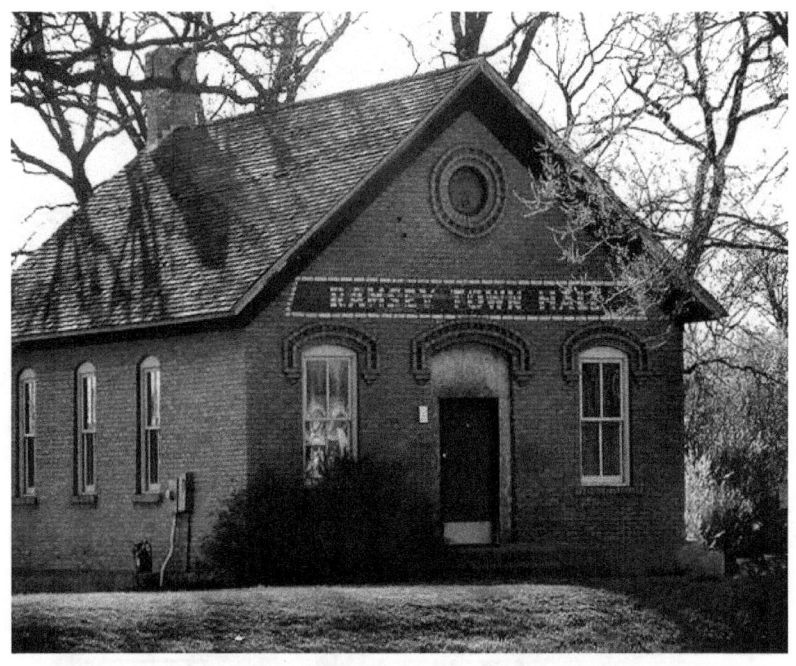

Here is the dam in Anoka MN shot while I was out walking one day.

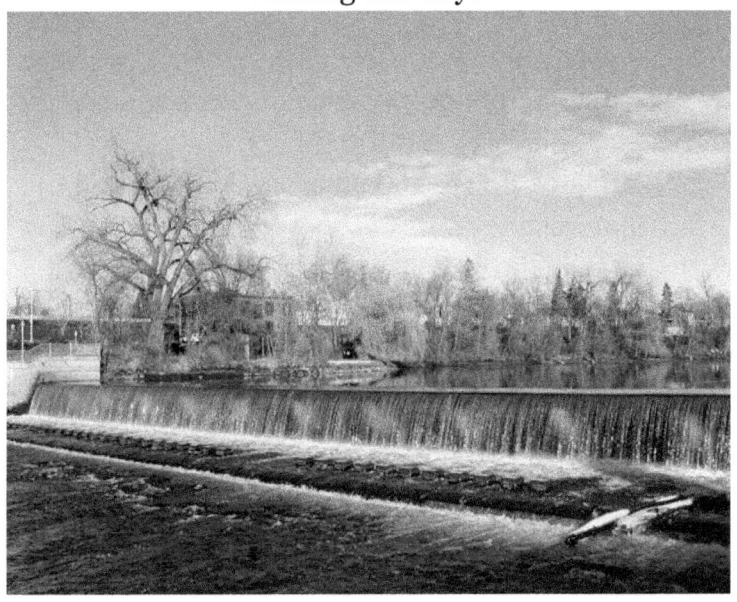

I could show you thousands of shots I would consider street photography; it is really anything you want it to be. The main thing is to look for great shots, find the right angle to shoot is and take the shots.

One other great tip for street photography if you are shooting person on the street is to use burst mode on your camera so you will be sure you can get a shot or two that are clear and sharp.

Make sure you look closely at things when you are passing them. Look at doors, windows, signs, people, buildings, natural things. Make sure you look up; look down, and all around you to find the most interesting things to shoot. Rain or snow can make for good street photography shots as well.

The possibilities are endless; you just need to look, and see them, and shoot them.

Landscapes

One of the problems with taking landscape photos is that sometimes it is hard for the viewer to know what the subject is. Many times, you see something that looks cool and you want to take a picture of it, but it is so hard to show what the subject is without a sense of scale.

One good way to have the subject in your landscape photos stand out is with some type of foreground object. Many people use other people for that. You can also use anything else interesting as a foreground object. Even something on the ground like a big rock, etc. Whatever looks cool.

You can also use a person as the focal point of your landscape shot. You can put them in the center of the shot, or you can use the rule of thirds and have the landscape shot that you want to take all around them. The person will add to the shot.

You can even use yourself as the person in the shot if you have a good tripod and set it up on a self-timer. Make sure if you do that, you time yourself walking to the spot from the camera so you know how long it takes you to get from the camera to the shot position. That way you will be sure the shot comes out right.

Using a person in your landscape shots, to add a sense of scale sometimes works well, everyone knows about the size of a person. If you have something big that you are trying to shoot a picture of, and you do not have anything to scale it to, it does not really do it justice. If you put a person next to it, the person gives a sense of scale to the photo and shows how big the object really is.

Another trick is if you add a sense of movement to the person, like they are jumping or walking, it adds interest to the shot. Another good thing to add interest is you can have them use a prop of some sort, like a colorful umbrella.

Another trick to use if you are using something natural is to get low so you get a good shot of the object in the foreground. I have thousands of examples of these tips, here are a few to show you what a difference it really makes.

This is a great shot across the valley to the mountains on the other side. This shot was taken at Bryce Canyon National Park in Utah. One of the most beautiful places I have ever seen.

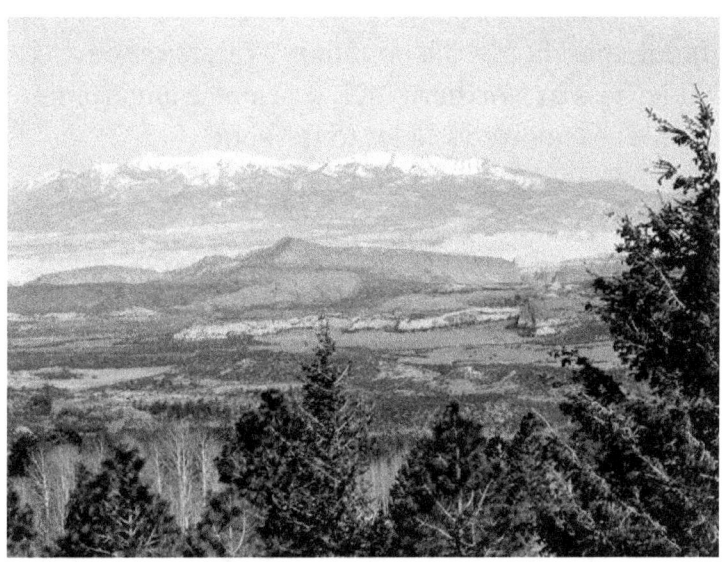

This shot is in Downtown St Paul MN. St Paul Cathedral. Flowers in front and framed by a tree on either side.

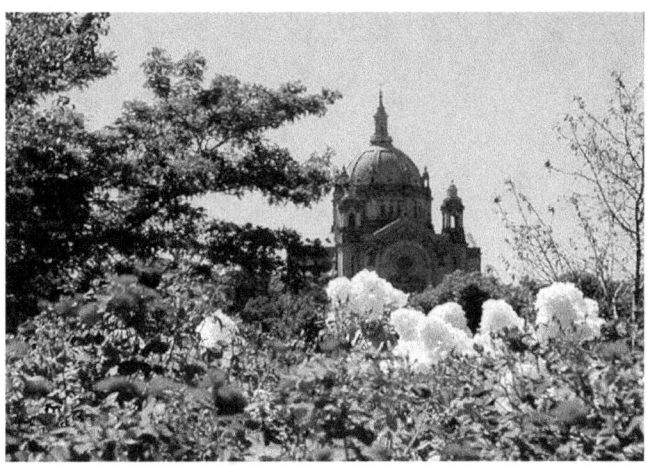

I took this shot in the boundary Waters canoe area wilderness in Northern MN. It is a nice landscape shot. The canoe adds a lot to the shot.

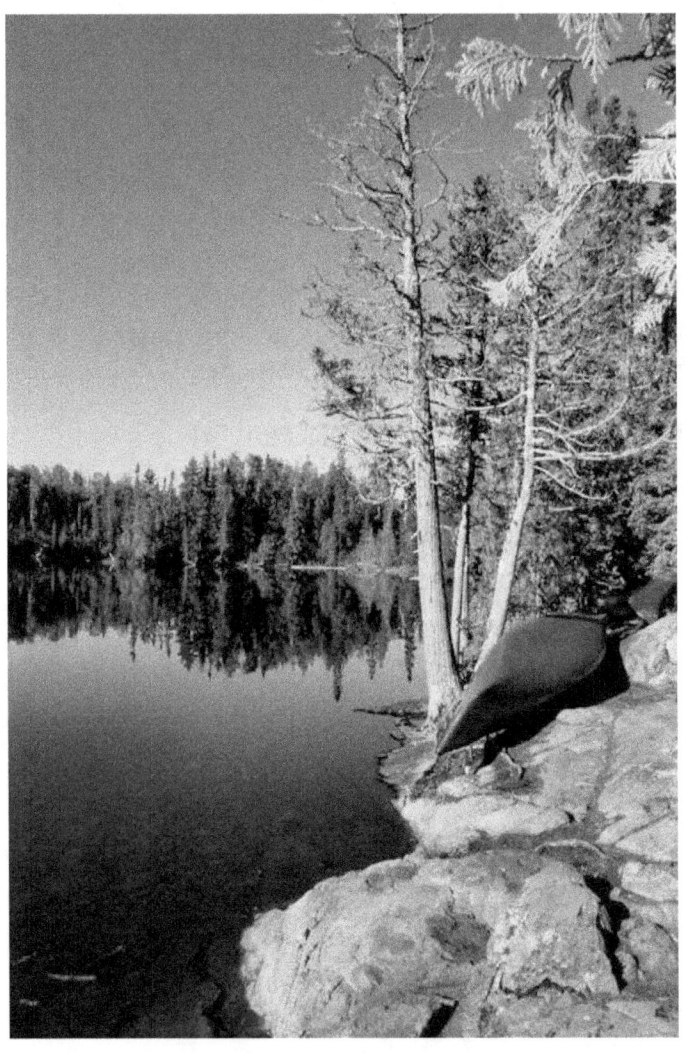

This is Split Rock Lighthouse on the North Shore of Lake Superior. Notice how the rock in the foreground adds interest to the shot.

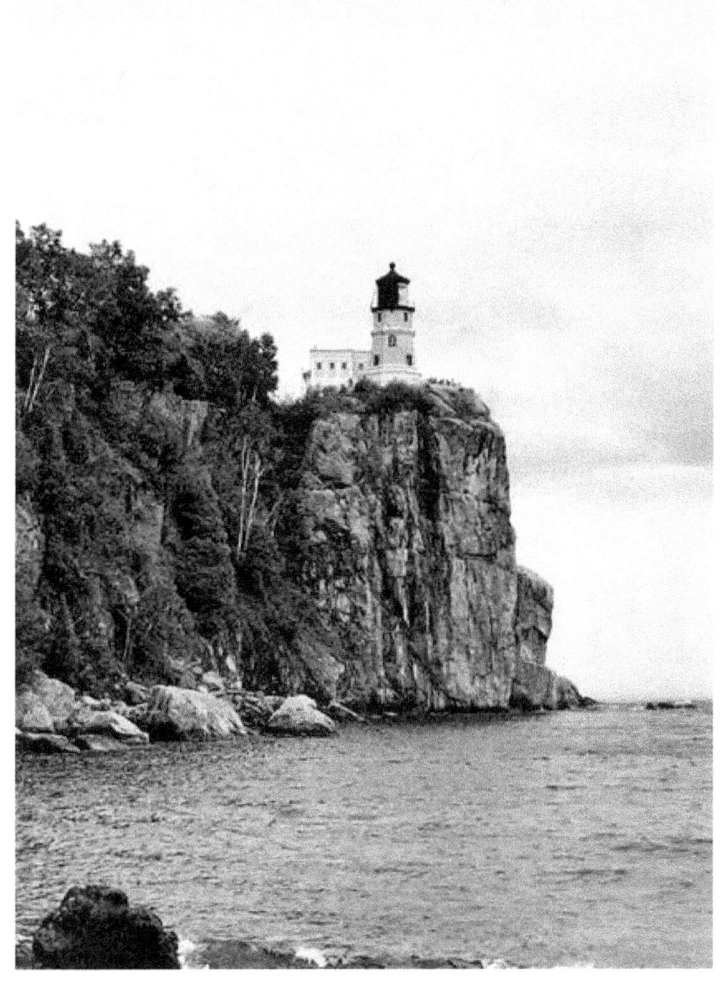

One more shot. Here is a shot in the U.P of
Michigan that I took at sunset on the shore of Lake
Superior. My wife in the shot adds scale and
interest to the shot.

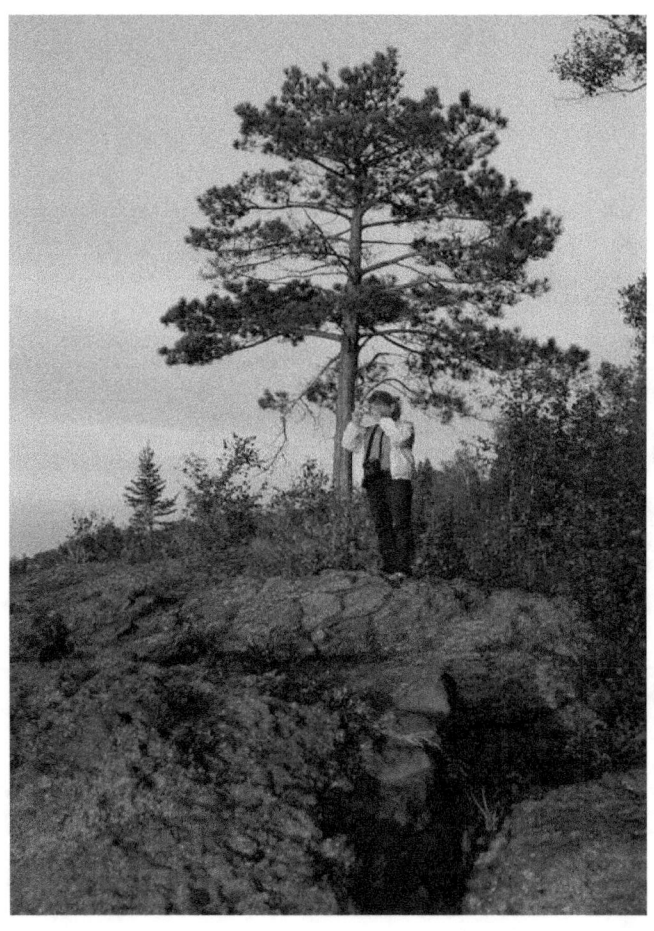

Portraits

Taking portraits with your iPhone is one of the most rewarding types of photos with an iPhone. One of the great things about shooting portraits is you do not have to worry about the subject being too far away. The process for taking great portraits is to first look at the lighting. Then determine what you want the shot to say, what the story of the shot is. Determine what you want for the composition. What things do you want in the picture, other than the subject?

Once you decide those things, get as close to the subject as you can while keeping your idea of the shot intact. Here is a portrait of my wife. When we are at the cabin, this is what she does. She sits on the dock and catches fish. Some genuinely nice fish. It is what she loves to do. Anyone that sees this shot and knows her knows this is a great shot portraying her.

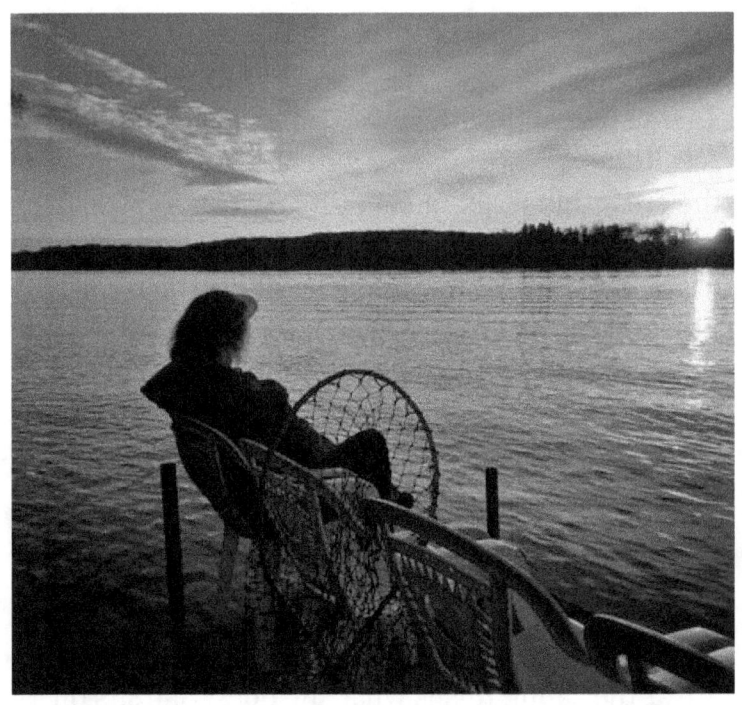

Here is a photo I took of my stepdaughter and her
husband. They did not know I was taking the shot;
it was a quick shot, spur-of-the-moment setup, and
shoot. It is a favorite of mine because of the great
colors and the leading lines; it was late afternoon on
an October day last year, so the sun was low in the
sky, and the whole shot works great.

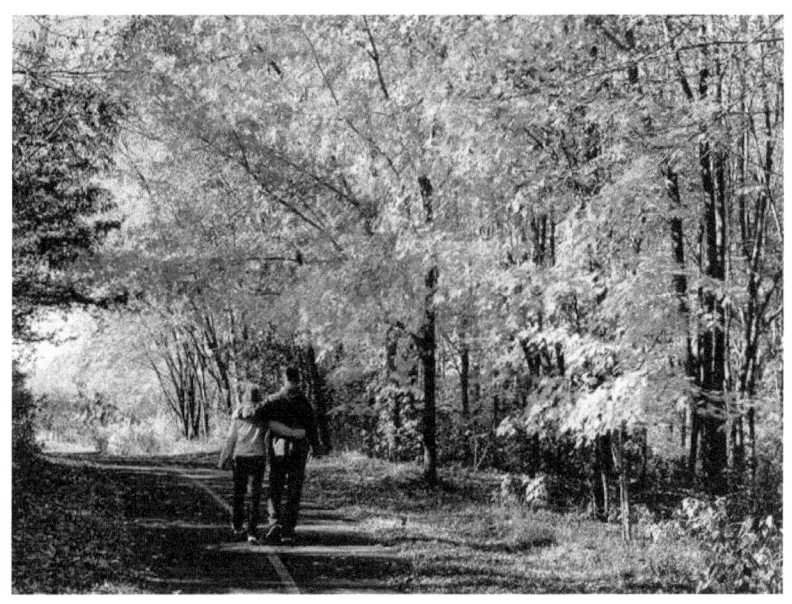

The keys to a great portrait are:

•Capture the subject doing something they love to do. A sport, a hobby, spending time with someone they care about. Etc. You want them to see the shot and have a reaction of I love that.

•Capture the beauty of the person with their eyes in the shot and sharp focus of the eyes.

•Make sure the subject, the person, is the focus of the shot. You can use people in landscape shots to give perspective, but if the shot is a portrait, do not have distracting objects in the background or foreground. You can take a landscape shot with your spouse in front of the Washington monument for scale, but do not take a portrait with the Washington monument as a background.

•Shoot from eye level of the subject.

•Shoot kids portraits of them in action. Let them do something they like, follow them around and keep taking shots while they are having fun.

•Compose the shot, then focus, not the other way around.

•Use a prop if the subject is nervous or cannot focus.

•Frame the subject to draw the viewer's eyes to the subject.

•When doing group portrait shots, always focus on the person closest to the camera. You do not want the first person seen to be out of focus.

•Leave space in the direction the subject is looking.

•Do not use the flash on your phone if you can help it.

•The shot can be part of the person. Even part of the face can make a great shot.

•Try to contrast the clothes and the surroundings.

Here are a few more examples of the tips above so you can see how the shot is better because of them.

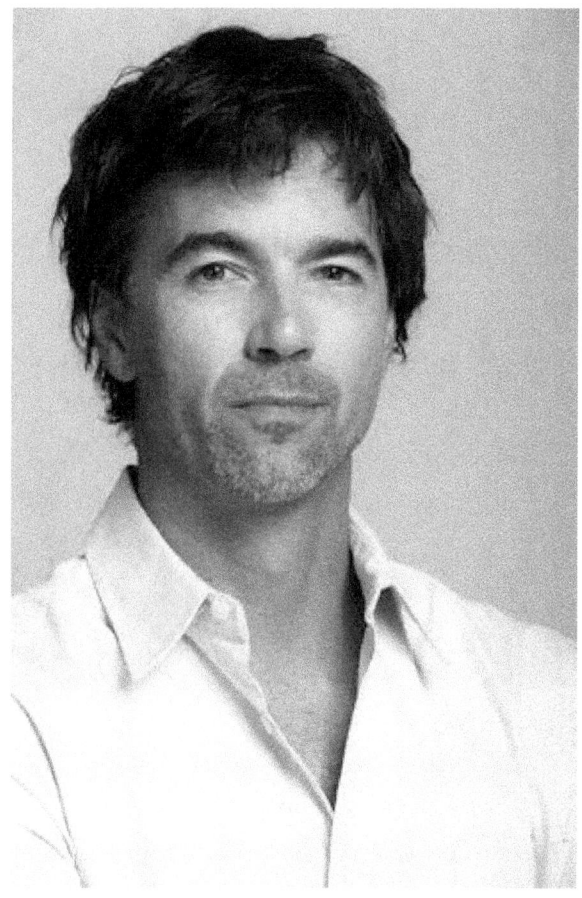

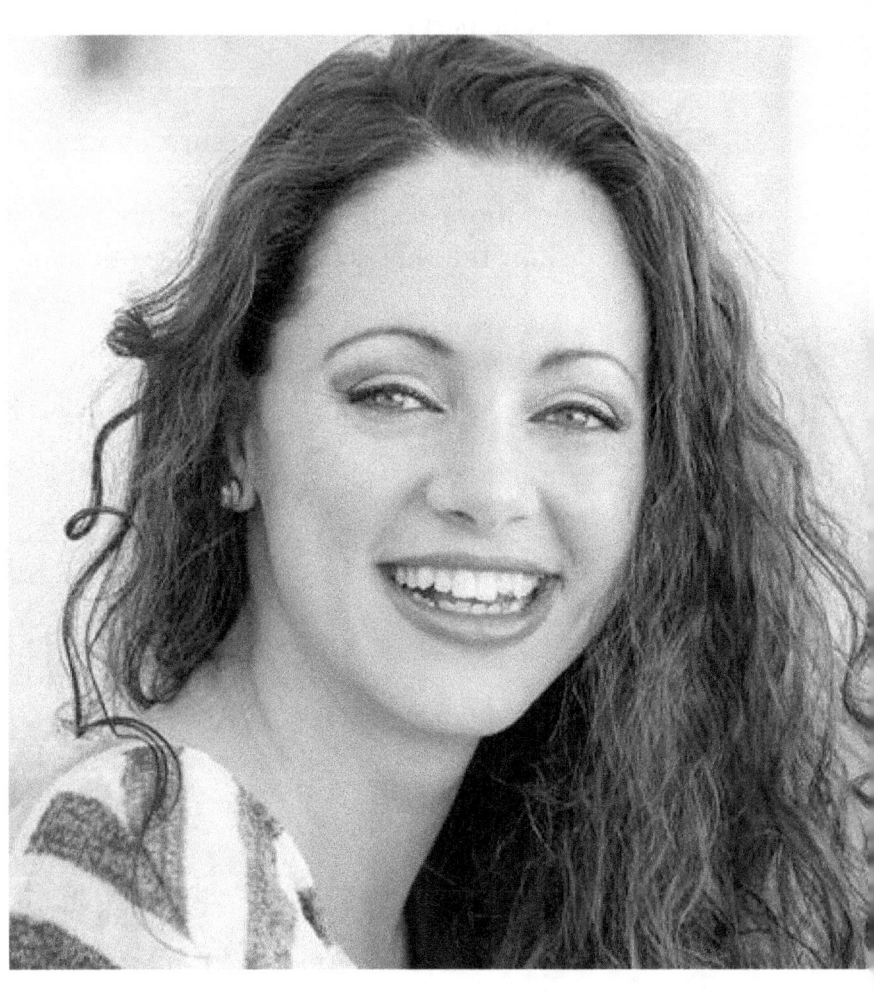

Nature

One of my favorite times to take nature and outdoor shots is in the fall. The bad thing about fall photography is the window for the best shots is short. You only have a couple weeks to a month to get the great shots.

 The biggest part of great fall photography is color. You need to get good vibrant colors in the shot. Multiple colors and good contrast will make them the best.

 Here is a shot I took last fall at the cabin. There is a lot of color and an interesting old outhouse that is the main subject of the shot. The fall colors and the overall atmosphere of fall ads a lot of interest to the shot.

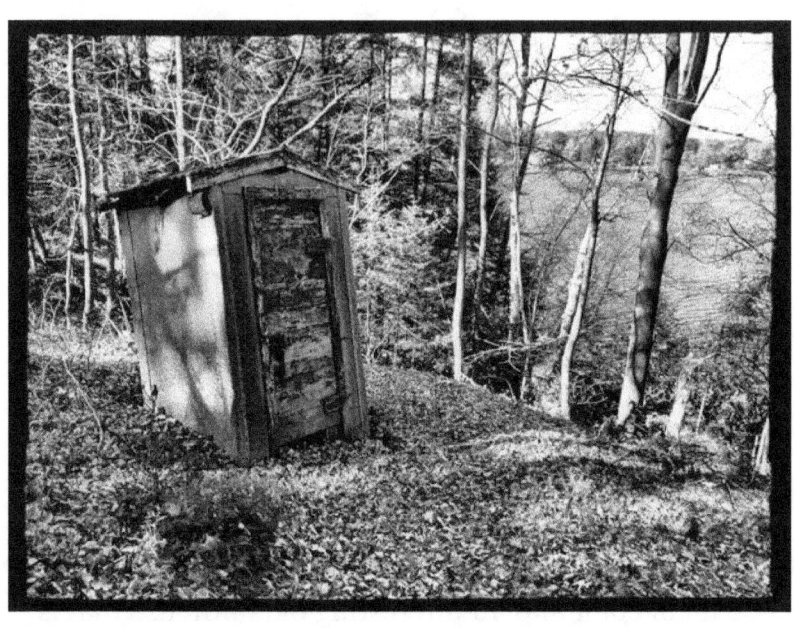

This is another nice fall shot that I took last fall. The subject of this shot is the clouds, but the lake and the fall colors in the background add to the overall shot.

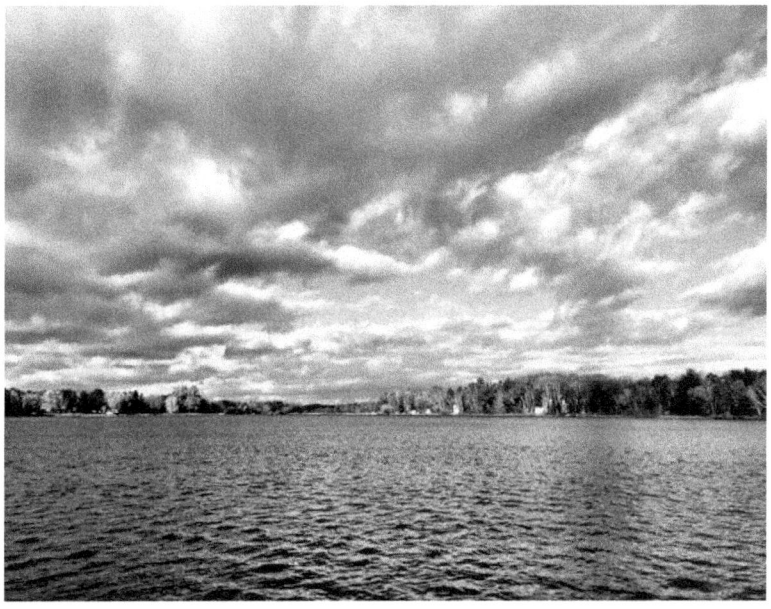

This shot was on Saturday morning; about 35 degrees, the fog had just lifted from the water, and made this fantastic image of the lake.

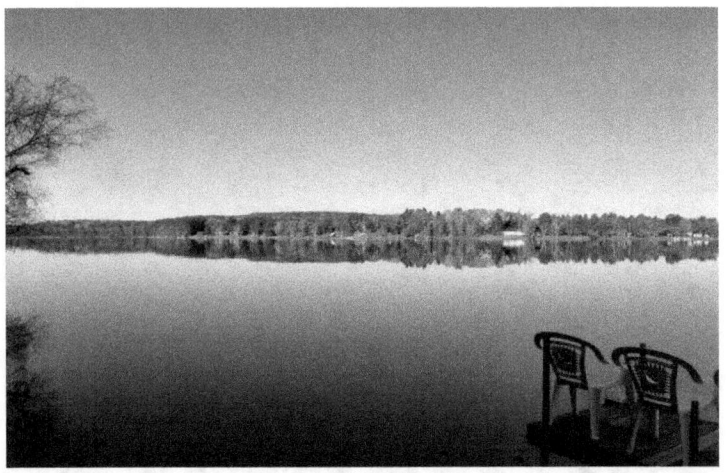

One more shot from the same area. This was in the yard at the neighbor's cabin. The barrel has been there for many years. It caught my eye as an interesting shot.

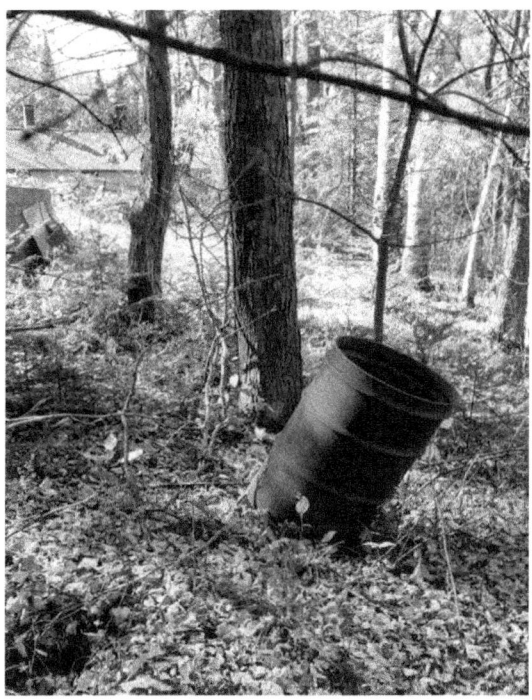

All four of these shots were taken within a short time. I just had to look to find them.

Looking for shots is how you will get your best ones. Most people do not look around them and they miss some of the most interesting and best things to look at. If you do your normal routine and do not try to see things, you will miss many of them.

I have seen that barrel many hundreds of times over the years, but normally I do not pay attention to it. As with most things we pass by, we do not really see them until we really look for good pictures.

Another great tip when shooting nature shots is to use a blue sky in your shot. It will give you great contrast and a perfect background that adds to the shot instead of taking focus away from the subject.

Another great tip for nature photography is to get in close when you can. The next shot shows how a lone mushroom growing on a piece of wood can be a great shot if you see and look at it and determine the best angle and the best positioning for the picture.

I literally have tens of thousands of more shots I can show you, I love taking nature shots; it is one of my favorite and relaxing things to do.

Using weather conditions and clouds to make the shot more dramatic is also something that works great in nature shots. Just be careful that you do not go too far and make it look overdone or fake.

Using post processing to make the shot more dramatic without making look fake is an art form, and it takes time and practice to be able to do it well. It is worth the trouble to learn to do it well.

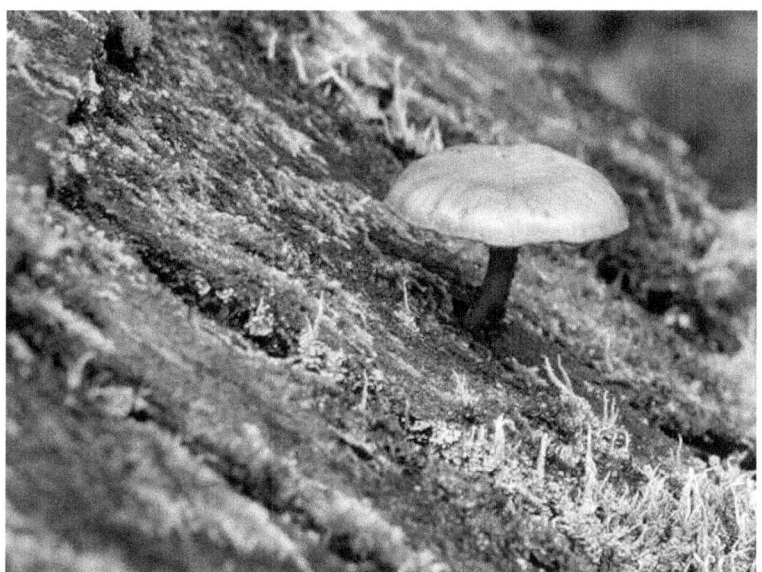

Techniques

Travel photos

Taking your travel photos with a DSLR will generally help you make better photos, but an iPhone can do a great job. The best thing about taking travel shots with an iPhone is that you always have it with you. Not lugging around a bulky heavy DSLR can also help you have more fun while traveling.

Make sure your lens is clean before you start to shoot. If the lens has a fingerprint on it, all the once in a lifetime shot you take will be blurry and not fixable.

Find the right exposure for the shot you are taking. It is normal to want the person you are on the trip with to be part of the shots. Do not get carried away with this type of shot. Do not put your spouse in front of every scenic place you see. If you are the only one that is ever going to look at the shots, and you want them in every shot, then go ahead.

If you want to be able to show your shots to other people and have them think it is a great shot, do not do it, if you want the shot to be special to you, then it is good. This shot is one of my wives at the lake; this one is just for me because I love to see her doing what she loves to do.

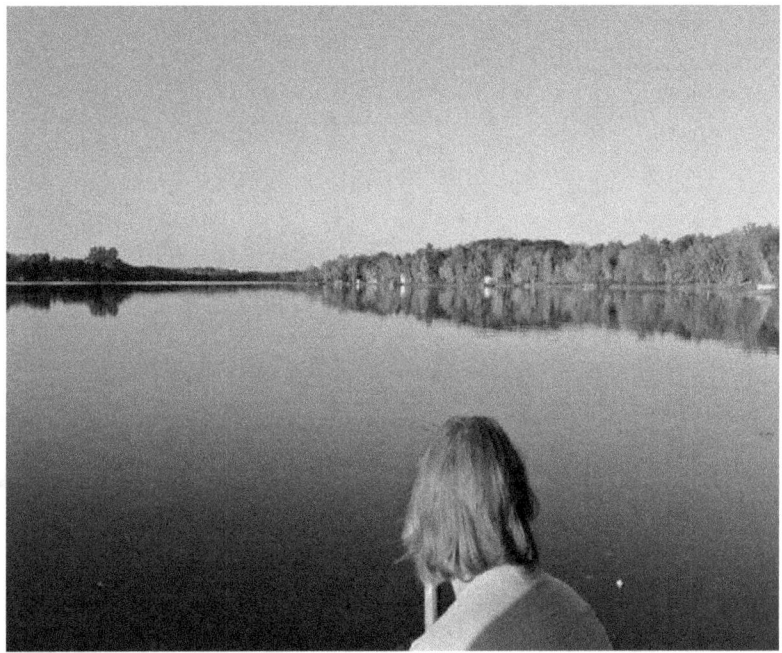

This is one of my favorite travel shot I have ever taken. It is in the U.P. of Michigan. I feel everything came together perfectly in this shot. I made a big canvas print of this shot and it hangs on my office wall.

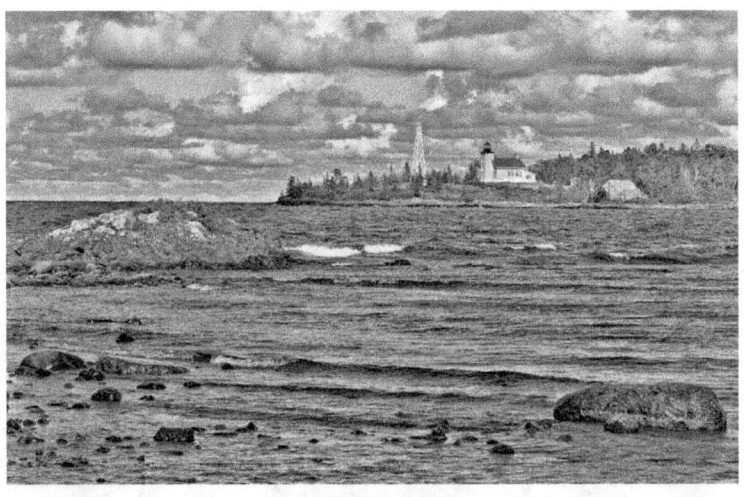

Here is another shot from the U.P. of Michigan. Again, the shot is better without a person in it, but I have the trees in the foreground to add interest.

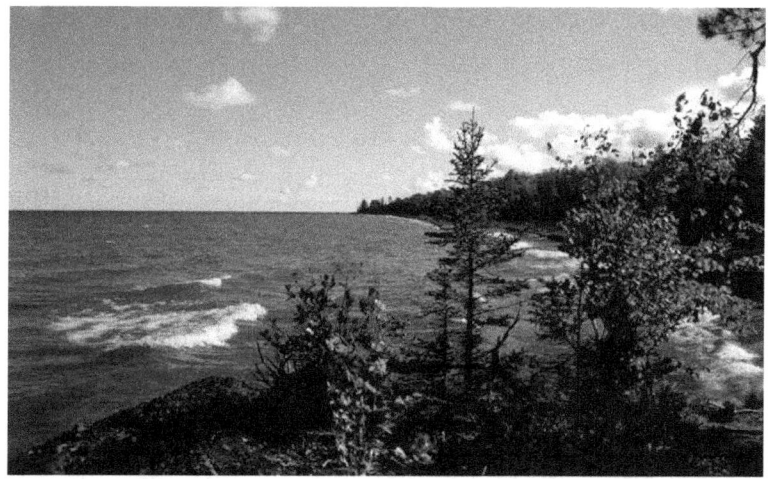

Another key to good travel photos is to take lots of shots. Some of them will not be great but many of them will. The more shots you take, the more likely it is that you will have tons of great shots.

Also use the special shooting modes for special shots. The panorama mode takes some cool shots. And if you really want to take cool panorama shots, take your time, you are moving the camera.

Long Exposure

One of the most interesting uses of long exposure shots is to make water look blurry. This shows motion, showing motion in your shots will add to the look of the shot.

The first thing you need to do on long exposure photography is to get a good tripod, or something you can set the camera on that is solid and will not move. It is terribly difficult to hold the phone still enough to not blur the picture hand holding the camera. That is no longer true. With my iPhone 11 I can hold still enough to take shots like this without a tripod. Any shutter speed slower than 1/15 sec is extremely difficult to do handheld, although the newer phone cameras are making it much easier.

Here is the perfect example of a long exposure waterfall shot.

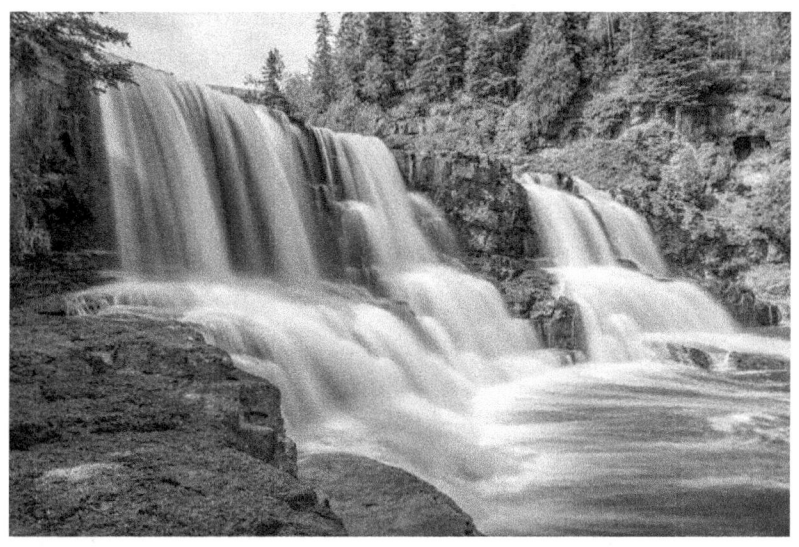

Attaching your phone to the tripod is still recommended if you can. The best mount I have found is Reticam adaptor. I got mine from Amazon. Here is a link to the page. This is a good solid mount. It costs more than most, but it is worth the cost.

The other thing that is very great to have is a Bluetooth remote to take the shot, so you don't have to touch the phone to take the shot. Here is the one I use that works very well. This is well worth the $7. You can also use the volume control buttons on the earbuds that come with the phone.

 To be able to keep the shutter open for long exposure, you need to get an app that fools the phone. What they do is combine multiple exposures into one. There are several apps that do this. I think the best is slow shutter cam. The app is free. Well worth it.

 Go into the settings and play around with it to get the best look. You can set the app for what type of shot you are taking so it can get the best shot for you. General settings that work best will be medium or high blur strength and a capture duration of 4 to 30 seconds.

 Because of the way the app works, this technique is easier to do with an iPhone that it is with a DSLR. You do not have to worry about using filters in daylight to get the exposure right for the rest of the scene. You still need to be careful of overexposure, but it is not hard to do.

 Any landscapes that include moving water are a great place to use this app and technique. Light trails and other low light situations are also great uses for this app.

Low light photos

Taking shots in exceptionally low light can be a challenge. The iPhone works great down to certain point, and then it does not work well without some special techniques.

Here is an example of what the iPhone does on its own and what the slow shutter cam can do.

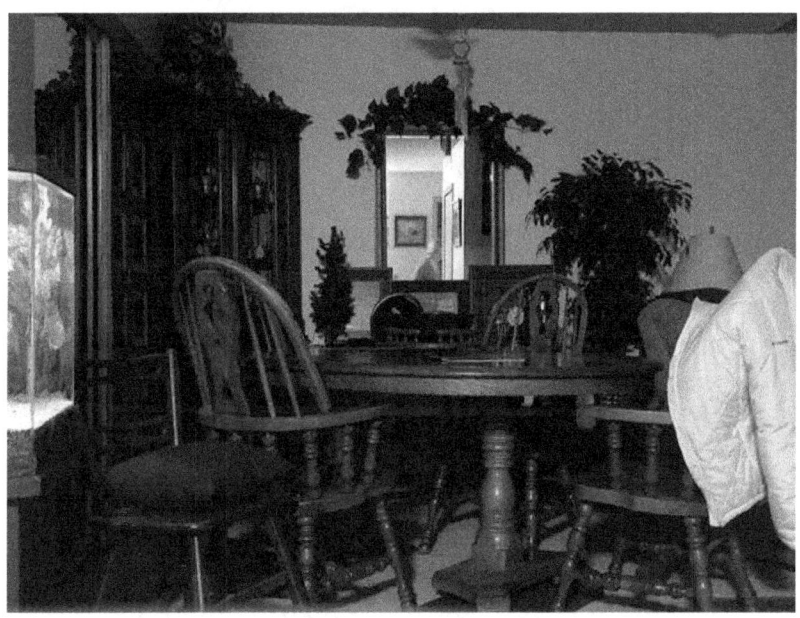

iPhone setting automatically.

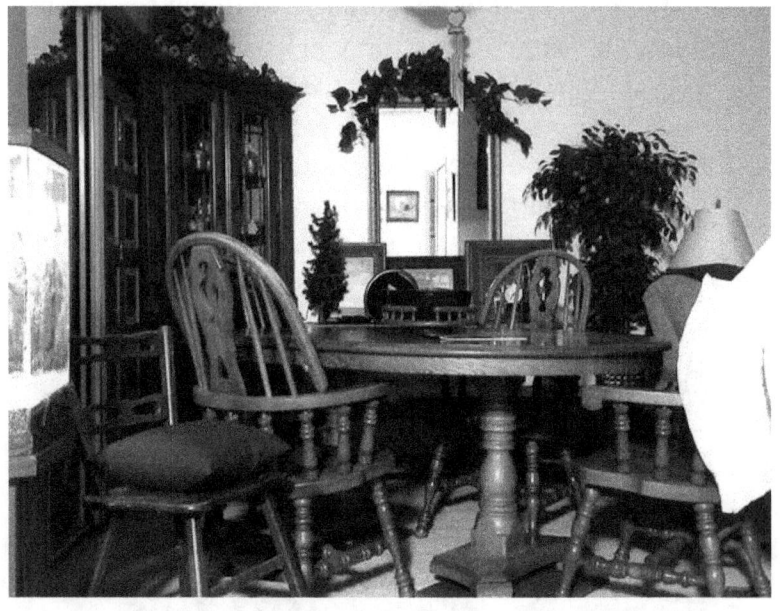

Slow shutter Cam with shutter speed set at 1/4 sec.

First, holding the phone steady is important. A tripod and remote release are important. Use the equipment mentioned above for best results. Also use the app slow shutter came from above.

If you have a light source, silhouettes can be great in low light areas. Use whatever light source you have to your advantage in low light shots.

Another very cool thing you can do with the Camera+ app works great for close shooting. You can tap on the flash icon and turn on your flashlight mode with the camera and use it to light up your subject.

A good LED flashlight can also be used while taking the shots to get some really good results. Painting with light techniques also work well with low light shooting.

In post shot editing, use the HDR tool in Snapseed or other editing tools to bring out details that are lost if underexposed. This works surprisingly well with many dark shots.

Using filters in Snapseed and other apps can also be used to alter the shot into something you may have never even thought of when you were taking the shot. The point of this is, do not delete any shot you think is junk until you try to fix it or filter it. You can get some cool shots out of something you initially thought was junk.

This section was updated for current phones.

On the newer iPhones there is an option for shooting shots in low light that is fantastic. You can take handheld shots in extremely low light and the shots come out good. Open the camera and get to where it is a low light situation. On the top of the screen next to the flash setting, there is a circle with lines going across it. Tap in it to activate it and it will show you the time for the shutter to be open. You can set it longer if you want. Just hold still and the pictures will come out great.

Slow shutter cam is still good for motion shots, but the newer iPhones will do much better with the built-in feature below.

I have an iPhone 11 now and I am blown away by how good the camera is. The anti-shake technology they are using, and the low light capabilities are unbelievable on these new iPhones. Here are a couple of shots I took in extremely low light.

The first shot I took was at 2 am in my basement with just a light in in the office to the left side of the room. It was very dark. The exposer time was 3 seconds.

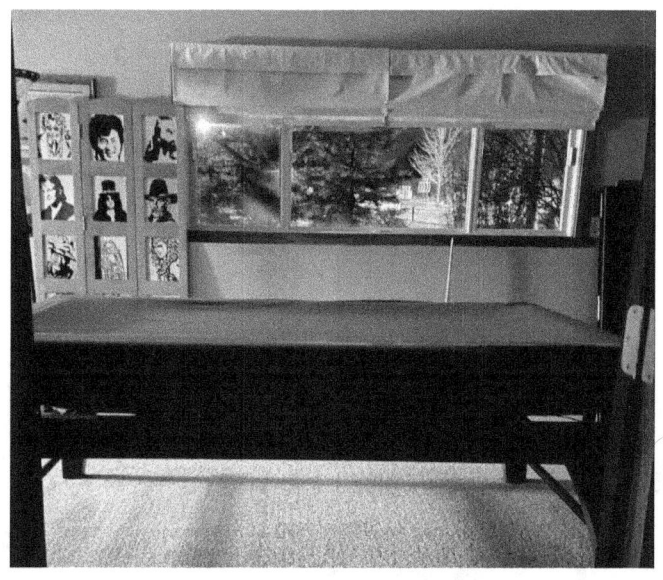

As a comparison, here is the same shot taken in regular mode with normal exposure with my iPad.

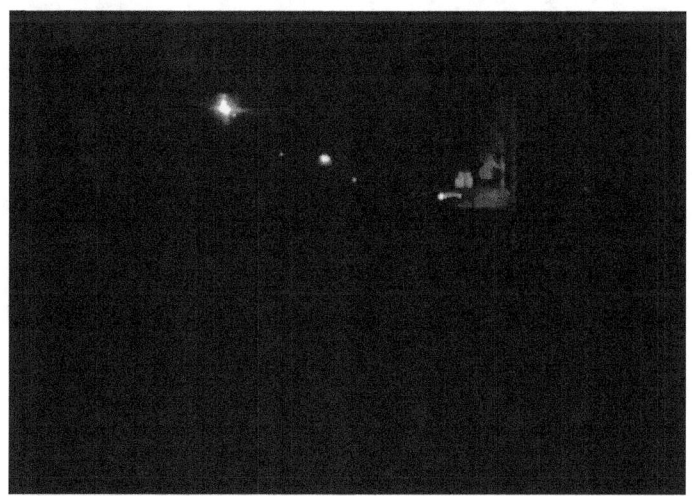

This one is taken out that window a couple of minutes later. These are just to see what you can do with this camera. It is amazing. The exposure on this was 3 seconds also.

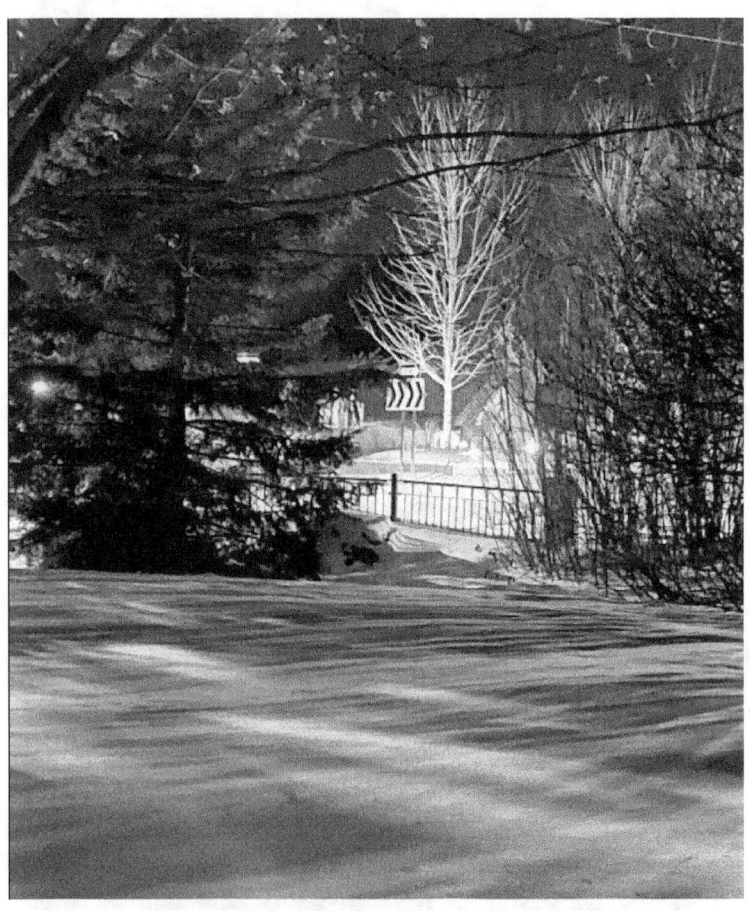

The time lapse and the slow motion are also cool. Try out all the options on these newer phones. Not only will your people photos be better, but you can also experiment with lots of artistic shots to make great photos. I have taken thousands of low light shots over the years and taking any handheld with an exposure of less than 1/15th of a second is nearly impossible.

Using negative space

Some shots can be dramatically improved with the use of negative space. What that means is having the subject in a good spot in the shot, with lots of blank or space with no detail in it.

You can also blur the entire background except the subject and use the blurred area as negative space. Use the negative space to emphasize what is important in the shot. Water and sky are the main things you can use for negative space in outdoor shots. For indoor shots, large blank walls work well.

Negative space is also a great way to add context to the shot, this will help you tell a story with the shot. If you take a close shot of a subject without the negative space, the viewer has nothing to relate the subject too. Telling a story with a photo needs to have something to relate the subject with so the viewer knows what the story is.

Empty space is also a great way to show the scale of a shot, something for the viewer to relate to and get a perspective of the shot.

Sometimes exaggerating the negative space will add to the look. Having the subject small and isolated in the shot can be a great technique.

Reflections

There are several types of reflection photos. You can use windows, water, mirrors, shiny floors, sunglasses, shiny tabletop, the screen of a television, phone, or tablet, or you can even us an app that gives you very realistic reflection shots.

Water is the most used reflective shot prop, but widows can give you some great ways to do the shots. You can mostly do this a few different ways. The reflection of the sunset on the water is the subject of the shot, it also adds much to the shot.

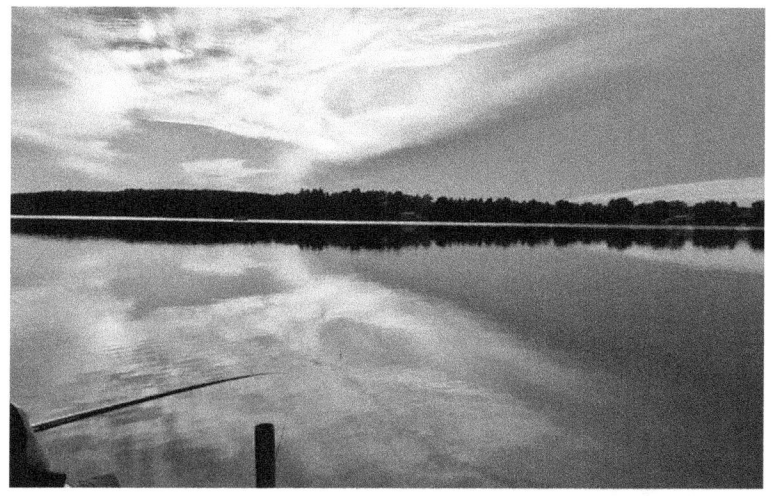

 You can show the subject with a background
reflection on the window.

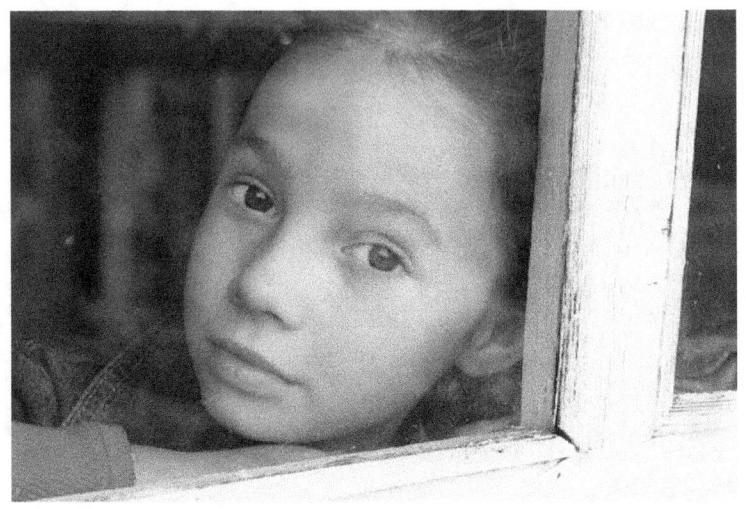

You can show the background with the subject reflected in the window.

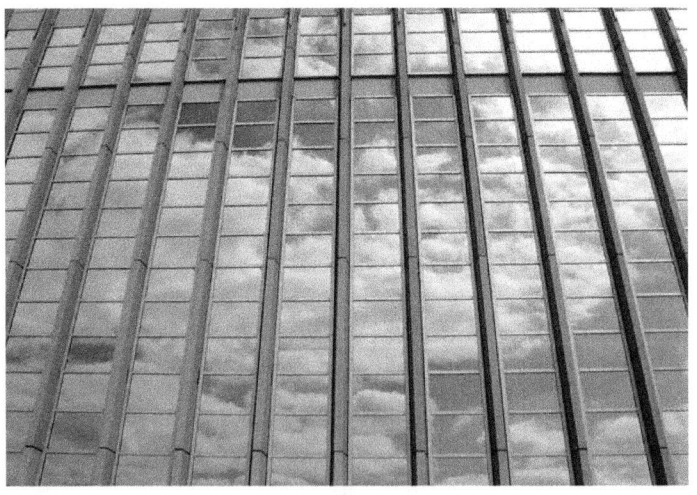

You can show the subject through the window, with the background reflected on the window.

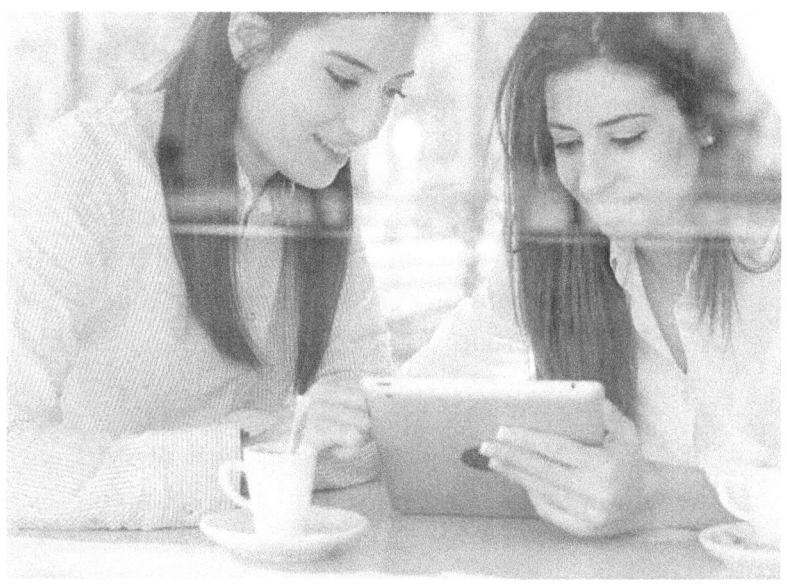

The first step is to find a reflective surface that you want to use for your shot. Look at the angles and options to take best advantage of the surface. If you are near a lake that is calm, you can find something that will make a great reflective shot with a big body of water.

You do not have to have a big body of water. Even a puddle or a wet dark surface after a rain can work great as well. Using a prop will often make the shot more interesting. Umbrellas are a great prop to use with the Wet Street or parking lot for interesting reflective shots.

On a body of water, looking for a reflection of objects you cannot even see in the shot can add a lot to the shot.

Using the reflect app gives you a lot of creative options with your shots. You can add a reflection to any picture and totally create something that never existed. Here are a couple of shots that I have added water too and a reflection for a totally new look.

I took this shot when the lake was very wavy, and the wind was blowing. I used the reflect app to make the water calm. Get the app at the app store. Reflect.

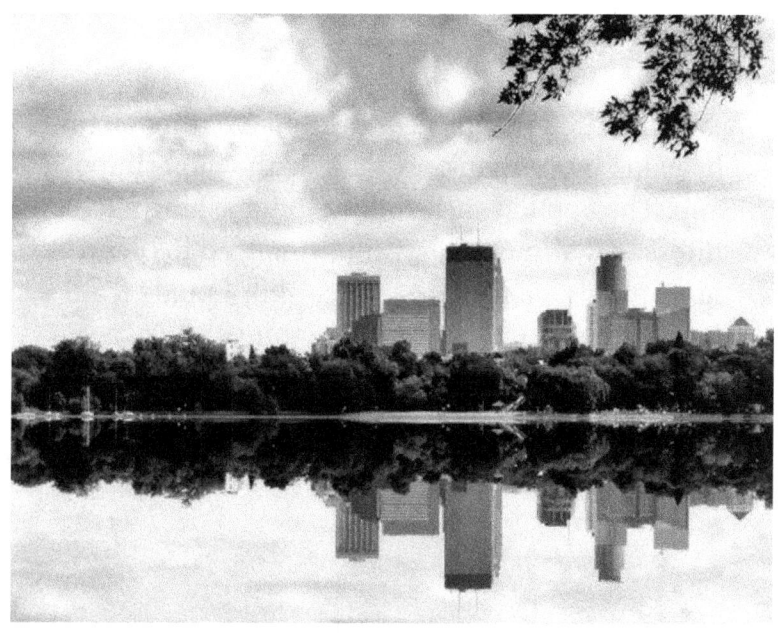

There are lots of options in the app. Check it out and play with it and see all the cool things you can do.

Fantasy shots

My favorite app for blending and creating pictures by using more than one photo is the Superimpose app. The app has incredibly good masking and filters and almost everything you need to blend multiple shots. Here is a quick shot I made from 3 photos that shows some of the things you can do.

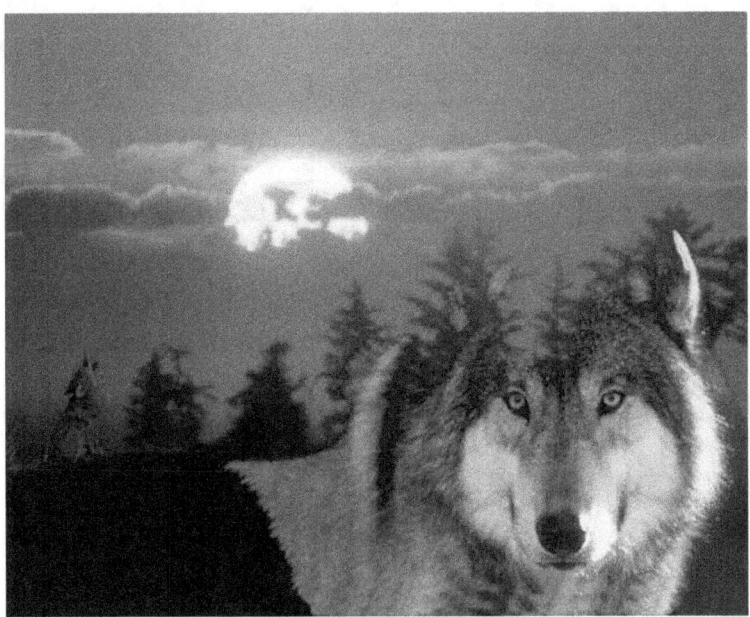

With a bit of imagination, there is not anything you cannot do with a little work.

Here is one more of a special shot I made from several other shots.

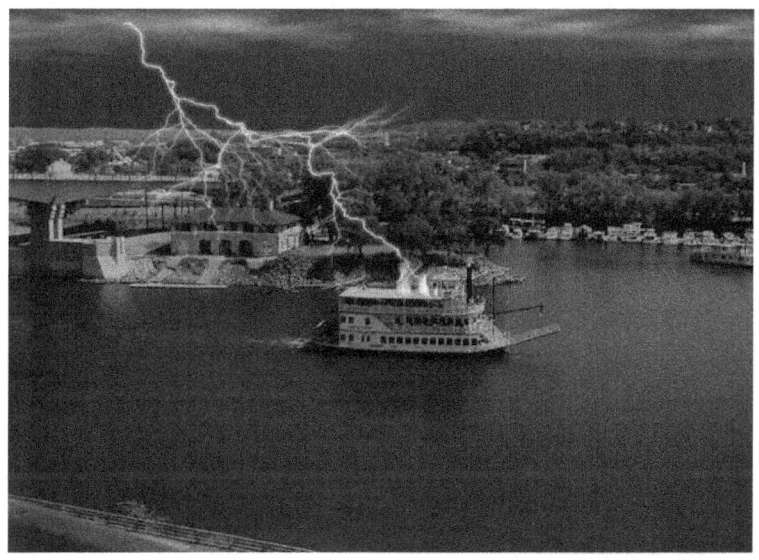

HDR Photos

This is one spot that the iPhone camera app itself makes a big difference. If you have the HDR turned on all the time when you are using the iPhone native app, you will get better pictures most of the time. The difference can be barely noticeable, or it can be significant. It all depends on the contrast and the lighting in the shot. If you are shooting on a bright sunny day, you will get better shots with HDR on almost every time.

Here is an example of the same shot taken at the same time, first one no HDR, the second one the HDR was on.

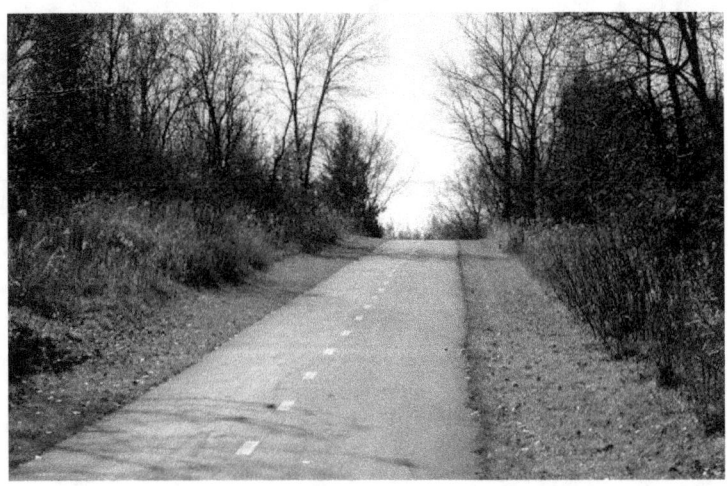

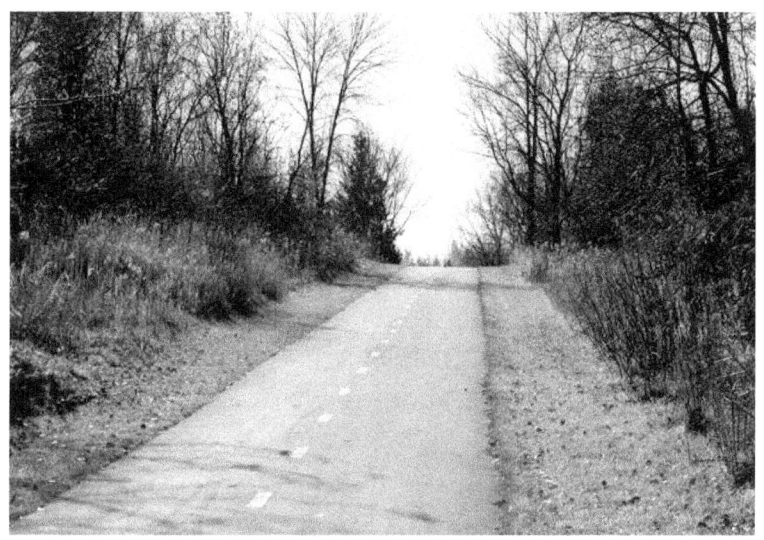

If you look at the two shots, the HDR shot is brighter, the colors a little more vibrant and the overall look of the shot is more pleasant.

There are many HDR options on almost every photo app that is available as well. Like I have said before, my favorite app to take shots and edit them is Camera+. This app has some great HDR filters as well as adjustments. You need to experiment with the apps to find out what you like the best, but as you can see, the iPhone app does an admirable job of improving the shot.

Remember that the iPhone will take 3 shots with different exposures and then combine them for the best shot. If you do the HDR editing after the shot, the app plays with the exposure and creates shots and blends them. Most of them do a good job but the iPhone app takes 3 shots.

Black and White

Most black and white shots are shot in color and converted to black and white. There are options with apps that will let you shoot in black and white, but if the shot does not look good in black and white, you have no option. It could be a great color shot.

Pay attention to the background when shooting black and white or color, but more so in black and white. Also pay attention to shapes and shadows to add to your shots.

High contrast is in my opinion a key in black and white. A flat looking gray shot will not be interesting.

Use all the same composition techniques that work in color photos. Rule of thirds, leading lines patterns, and textures. Texture stands out more in black and white than it does in color.

High contrast in the sky with clouds can add a lot to black and white shots. A bright blue sky is great for color landscape shots, but a stormy cloudy sky looks much better in black and white. To make great black and white shots, you need to learn to see in black and white. Seeing these things will make your black and white shots better.

Converting color shots to black and white

You want to have shots with light areas and dark areas. These types of shots make the best black and white photos.

Here is a shot that I took with good contrast and cool looking clouds.

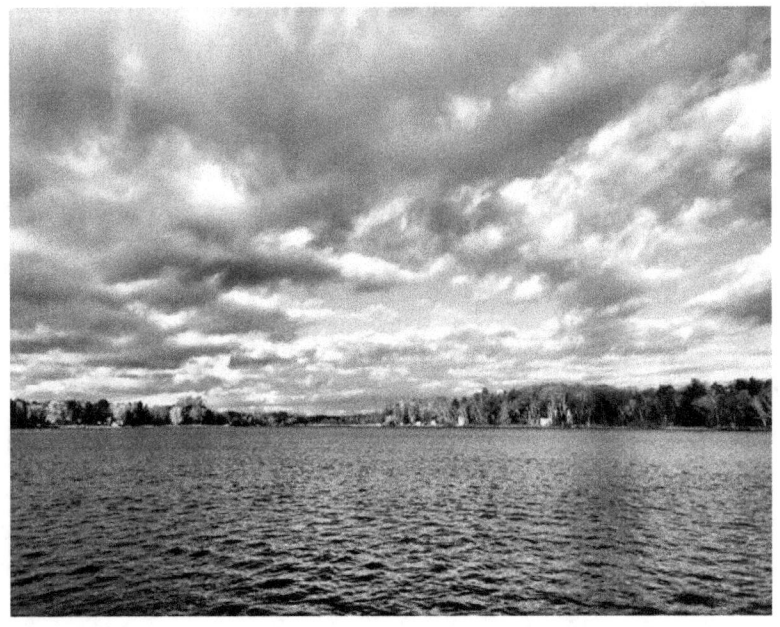

I opened the shot in the app Tadaa, and all I did
was desaturate it, increased the contrast a little and
then opened the easy HDR and tweaked it slightly.
This is how it looks now.

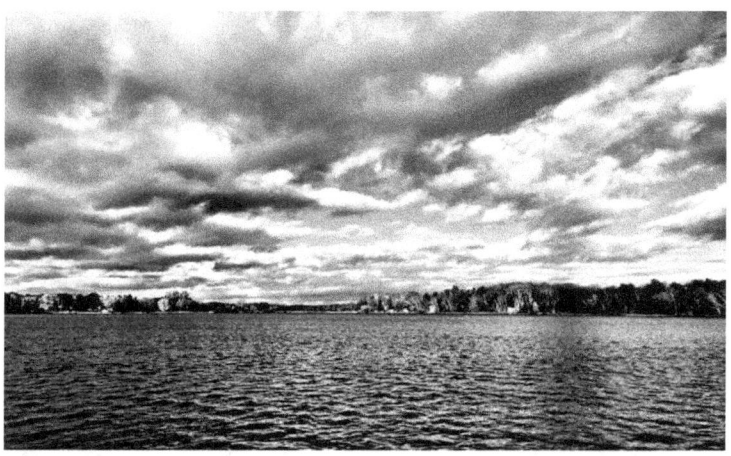

This is likely much more dramatic than most people would like, but this is just an example of what you can do.

If you start with a shot that you know is going to look good as black and white it is easy. Many apps have a black and white conversion filter or several that do a good job as well. Dramatic in black and white is normally better.

Picks play pro I think is the best and easiest to convert your shots. It has an entire section of black and white filters that use the color channels as well as other options.

This example I did in Picks play pro; it literally took me about 15 seconds. I just loaded the shot, selected fx studio, went to black and white went to red channel and it was done.

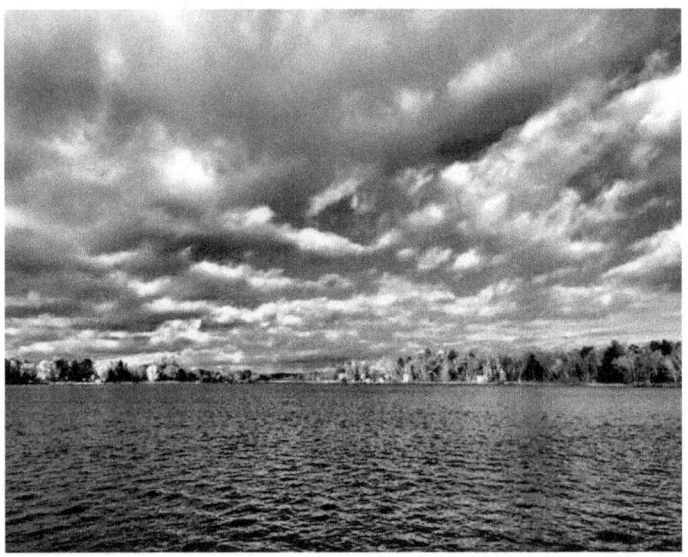

Specialty Shots

One of the cool specialty shots you can do with an iPhone is time-lapse. What time-lapse does is take a shot a set duration and then puts the shots together into a sort of video.

You can shoot things like taking a shot every several minutes of a flower that is opening. When put together it looks like a video that shows the whole process of the flower opening. The best subjects for time-lapse are things that happen slowly over time.

This is not a type of photography that you are going to use often, but you can get some cool shots with the right subject and set up.

A key is the camera cannot move for the duration of the time-lapse. You need a good tripod or the bracket that I use. This bracket can stand up on a flat surface while holding your phone without a tripod or can be attached to a tripod.

The time-lapse feature on the iPhone has built in setting that will drop frames from the video the longer you shoot. This makes it look natural without making it go too slow. The longer the shoot the faster the video will play back.

Try it and play around with it, you can have some fun with it.

A new feature on the 6s and 6s plus is the 3D touch. What this does is take a short video of the shot and makes it move when you view it, so it looks like an animated GIF. On the newer model phones, it is the live shooting. The subjects of the shot need to be moving, not the phone, keep the phone still. Keep in mind these shots will take up a lot more space in your memory. They are cool but use them sparingly to save space. The phone will even let you set a 3D touch shot as your wallpaper.

Attachments

One of my favorites add on things for the iPhone, or any camera phone is my Bluetooth shutter button. I use this many times in lots of situations. You can set the phone on a counter or anywhere solid. You can stand back and take shots of a subject or use it to take selfies.

The button will work from up to 30 feet from the camera. You can hold it at your side or behind your back, so it is not part of the shot. It is also very inexpensive.

It works great if you have the phone on a tripod, or even holding it in your hand. It is hard in low light situations to use the volume or tap the screen without moving the phone at all. Using this button will allow you to take the shot without moving the camera at all.

<u>**Here is the link to the button on Amazon.**</u>

Another key adds on item that I think is needed is a phone holder. I have tried several, this is the one that is the best.

This piece is a one of the more expensive holders, but it is the best. It is made from steel and is very solid. It is not liked the spring-loaded cheaper ones; this will never drop your phone. It will hook to any tripod, and if you just set it on a counter, it will hold the phone without a tripod.

Here is the Amazon link.

Another item that I use often is this mini tripod with flexible and bendable legs. You can move it at any angle or turn it almost any way you will need to get the shot you are looking for. The one I use is no longer available. Here is the page on Amazon with the mini tripods. Pick one that will work good for your use.

Add on lenses. I am sure there are several lenses that work well with a smartphone camera. What I have found is the sets from Olloclip offer the best quality, but they are much costlier than some of the other sets of lenses you can get.

You can buy them directly from their website.

Editing

Most of the shots you take with your iPhone will need a little editing to look their best. You will probably only need to tweak the exposure and enhance the colors. If you want to edit shots taken from the iPhone app, or if you want to further edit shots you have saved, these are the apps that I use.

Snap seed is probably the most powerful app that I have found for just editing. It has a full range of editing options. The app has lots of filters and adjustments to let you set almost anything in the shot. This app does let you take shots in the app, but the camera does not have many settings.

Most of the great things you can do in this app are for after you take the shot with a different app. It has some great features. Almost everything is adjustable in the Snap seed app. It has full adjustments on every part of the shot. It is also loaded with filters and other special effects that you can use to enhance your photos as well as all the normal adjustments you can do with any good photo editor.

Photo Editing workflow

Open the photo in Snapseed photo editor.

The first thing to do is crop the photo to what you want left in the shot.

Second thing I do is to adjust the exposure and lighting. Generally, the shots need some work on the sky. I generally darken the sky and lighten the land.

You can even use masks in this program.

Adjust any other pieces that need to be tweaked and sharpen last if needed.

The other main app that I use for editing photos is Be funky.

Be Funky

When I use the Apple app, I generally edit the shots in Be Funky. The app is extremely easy to use and gives you good choices and good results. Be Funky is an app that also has an online photo editor that you can use on your computer.

Open the Be Funky app and select Photo Editor. Then tap the image icon in the top middle and select the picture you want to work on. The picture will come up on the screen, select use photo.

Pick one of the options on the bottom and look at the different options in each one. A quick and easy way to make your shots instantly much better is to tap edits, then slide over to beautify. Tap on that tile and use the slider to give your shot some pop.

Play with some of the other options; this is a powerful and easy program for someone who has never edited photos. It is also great for people who know more about editing. It is quite simple and effective.

You can also use this app to make a Collage of multiple photos if you want to send more than one and do not want to use so much data.

Another powerful editing app I would recommend trying is Visionn. This app is cool in that it lets you take your shot in a kind of cartoon looking mode. It is not for everything, but you can make some cool looking photos.

Picsplay is one more that I use and would recommend. This app also has some things that I have not found in other apps, or they work better in this app. The interface is easy to use, and it has tons of filters. There is a picsplay 2 version also that I have not tried. The classic version does a lot.

There are so many apps out there, you just need to pic a couple and use them. The ones I mention here will do anything you want to do with your photos.

Inspiring photos

Here are some links to awesome photos that were all taken with an iPhone.

These links are some of the great sites I found that have some unbelievable photos taken with an iPhone that will give you inspiration to go out and take some awesome shots of your own. As you can see there is no limit to what you can do with your phone camera. These shots look they were taken with an SLR camera.

Wrapping it up

Taking great photos with your iPhone is not hard. The camera in the phone is good enough to take most of the shots you want to take. If you use photography tips and techniques that are used for taking all great photos, you will be right at home with an iPhone camera.

The iPhone has some unique features that you cannot get with many other cameras. There are also many apps that make using the iPhone camera much easier and better.

Once you learn what you can do with it, and the tricks to shooting the best photos you can with it, you will be able to take and show off pictures to your friends and family that will make them say WOW.

If you think you learned some valuable information from this book, I would be greatly appreciative to you if you **would go to the Amazon website and leave a review.** Reviews help show others that there is good useful information readily available that will help us all take the best shots that we can, with a device that we have with us all the time.

Thank you for reading my book.

www.ingramcontent.com/pod-product-compliance
Lightning Source LLC
Chambersburg PA
CBHW051327170526
45166CB00002B/708